AI

REVEALED

AI

REVEALED

Theory • Applications • Ethics

Erik Herman

MERCURY LEARNING AND INFORMATION
Boston, Massachusetts

Publisher: David Pallai
MERCURY LEARNING AND INFORMATION
121 High Street, 3rd Floor
Boston, MA 02110
info@merclearning.com
www.merclearning.com
800-232-0223

E. Herman. *AI Revealed: Theory • Applications • Ethics*
ISBN: 978-1-50152-333-5

The publisher recognizes and respects all marks used by companies, manufacturers, and developers as a means to distinguish their products. All brand names and product names mentioned in this book are trademarks or service marks of their respective companies. Any omission or misuse (of any kind) of service marks or trademarks, etc. is not an attempt to infringe on the property of others.

Library of Congress Control Number: 2024919785

242526321 This book is printed on acid-free paper in the United States of America.

Our titles are available for adoption, license, or bulk purchase by institutions, corporations, etc. For additional information, please contact the Customer Service Dept. at 800-232-0223 (toll free).

All of our titles are available in digital format at academiccourseware.com and other digital vendors. The sole obligation of MERCURY LEARNING AND INFORMATION to the purchaser is to replace the files, based on defective materials or faulty workmanship, but not based on the operation or functionality of the product.

To the dearly departed, now,
and forever one of the grateful dead.

CONTENTS

PREFACE

Welcome to *AI Revealed: Theory • Application • Ethics*, an exploration into the world of artificial intelligence (AI). This book aims to unveil the multifaceted domain of AI, a field that has transformed the landscape of technology and its interaction with human society. Whether you are a student, a professional stepping into the realm of AI, or a curious mind eager to understand the underpinnings and implications of this technology, this book is designed to cater to your intellectual curiosity.

AI today is not just a field of study; it's an integral and dynamic part of our daily lives. From the algorithms that curate our social media feeds to the sophisticated systems driving autonomous vehicles, AI's applications are vast and expanding at an unprecedented rate. However, the journey of AI from theoretical concepts to real-world applications is layered with intricate developments, challenges, and ethical debates.

This book begins with *Chapter 1*, offering an introduction to AI, including its definition, the various types of AI, and the core components such as machine learning, neural networks, robotics, and expert systems. We delve into the history of AI, tracing early concepts, key milestones, and the evolution of modern AI technologies.

In *Chapter 2*, we lay the foundations of machine learning, exploring essential concepts like supervised and unsupervised learning, and discussing model evaluation and selection methods. This chapter sets the stage for understanding how machines learn from data to make intelligent decisions.

Chapter 3 examines deep learning and neural networks, covering artificial neural networks, convolutional neural networks (CNNs), and recurrent neural networks (RNNs). We also touch upon advanced architectures like Generative Adversarial Networks (GANs) and Transformers, essential for understanding the cutting-edge developments in AI.

Chapter 4 introduces natural language processing (NLP), examining how AI understands and processes human language. We cover topics like text preprocessing, sentiment analysis, named entity recognition, and machine translation, showcasing AI's capabilities in interpreting and generating human language.

Chapter 5 focuses on computer vision, exploring the techniques used to enable machines to see and understand visual information. It includes topics like image preprocessing, object detection, image classification, and image segmentation, demonstrating AI's ability to interpret and interact with visual data.

In *Chapter 6*, we address the critical ethical considerations in AI, including issues of bias in AI algorithms, fairness, accountability, and the need for regulation and governance. This chapter emphasizes the importance of developing AI technologies responsibly to avoid unintended consequences.

Chapter 7 presents real-world industry case studies, showcasing AI's impact across sectors like healthcare, finance, transportation, retail, and manufacturing. We highlight both the potential and challenges of implementing AI technologies in these industries.

Chapter 8 looks ahead to the future of AI and emerging technologies. Topics such as quantum computing, edge AI, explainable AI, and AI for social good are explored, giving insight into the next frontier of AI innovation.

Chapter 9 serves as a practical guide for readers interested in AI development. It covers setting up a development environment, introduces Python for AI, and provides an overview of popular AI libraries, helping readers start their journey in AI programming.

AI Revealed is not just a textbook; it is a comprehensive guide to understanding and engaging with AI at multiple levels. It includes practical applications and hands-on projects, helping readers bridge theory with practice and apply AI creatively and ethically.

Join us as we embark on this journey, aiming to define AI, explain its workings, and explore how it can be harnessed responsibly to benefit humanity. Together, we will unfold the layers of AI as we step into a future where the fusion of human and artificial intelligence continues to shape new frontiers.

Acknowledgments

Without Grace Hopper, these are all just words in the wind. I acknowledge that on the minds and backs of too many great women and men to mention does this work come forth, so I pause and continue the work.

Erik Herman
October 2024

## CHAPTER 1

THE FOUNDATIONS OF ARTIFICIAL INTELLIGENCE

This opening chapter explores the realm of artificial intelligence (AI), starting with its definition and spanning its rich history, including the importance, and diverse applications. As AI continues to integrate into various facets of modern life, understanding its fundamentals becomes essential. This chapter lays the groundwork by introducing key concepts and terms, tracing the evolution of AI technologies, and discussing their transformative impact on society. This chapter also begins the exploration of the ethical considerations that underpin AI development and deployment, setting the stage for deeper discussions in later chapters.

FIGURE 1.1 A conceptual representation of AI.

Figure 1.1 illustrates a conceptual representation of AI, depicted as a human brain formed by interconnected circuits and glowing nodes. The intricate network symbolizes the complexity and interconnectivity of AI technologies, reflecting the integration of digital and cognitive processes that mimic human intelligence. This visual metaphor highlights the technological foundation of AI, emphasizing its role in processing information and generating intelligent behavior.

WHAT IS ARTIFICIAL INTELLIGENCE?

Artificial intelligence (AI) is the scientific field dedicated to creating machines capable of performing tasks that typically require human intelligence. These tasks include decision-making, language translation, visual perception, speech recognition, and problem-solving. AI encompasses a broad spectrum of technologies and methodologies aimed at building systems that can adapt to new inputs, learn from data, and improve over time without human intervention. The goal of AI research and development is to enhance the ability of machines to mimic cognitive functions and carry out complex tasks with efficiency and accuracy.

AI can be categorized into distinct types based on their capabilities and applications. *Narrow AI*, also known as *weak AI*, is designed to perform a specific task, such as facial recognition or language translation, and operates within a limited scope. In contrast, *general AI*, or *strong AI*, aims to replicate human intelligence and can perform any intellectual task that a human can. The most advanced form, *superintelligence*, refers to AI that surpasses human intelligence in all aspects, including creativity, problem-solving, and emotional understanding. Core components of AI include *machine learning*, which involves training algorithms on large datasets to make predictions or decisions, and neural networks, which are modeled after the human brain and enable deep learning and pattern recognition. Understanding these fundamentals is crucial for grasping the full potential and implications of AI in various fields.

Definition of AI

Artificial intelligence (AI) is defined as the capability of a machine or system to perform tasks that typically require human intelligence. These tasks encompass a wide range of activities, such as visual perception, speech recognition, decision-making, and language translation. AI systems leverage algorithms and statistical models to execute these complex functions. By processing vast amounts of data, they can identify patterns and make informed decisions, simulating elements of human cognitive function.

At its core, AI aims to mimic the human mind's ability to learn, reason, and solve problems. Through techniques like machine learning and deep learning, AI systems improve their performance over time as they are exposed to more data. This adaptability allows AI to handle increasingly sophisticated tasks, from recognizing faces in photos to translating entire documents across languages. Understanding these foundational aspects of AI is crucial for appreciating its potential to transform various industries and enhance everyday life.

Types of AI

AI can be categorized into three main types based on its capabilities and scope of function:

Narrow AI

Also known as weak AI, these systems are designed to handle a single or limited task. Examples include speech recognition, image recognition, and search engines. Narrow AI operates under a set of constraints and limitations, performing predefined functions without possessing consciousness or understanding. It excels at specific tasks but lacks the ability to perform beyond its programmed scope. Common applications include virtual assistants like Siri and Alexa, recommendation systems on streaming platforms, and autonomous vehicles.

General AI

These systems possess the capability to understand and learn any intellectual task that a human being can. This type of AI, also referred to as strong AI, is still largely theoretical and not yet fully realized in practical applications. General AI would require a machine to have the same cognitive abilities as humans, including reasoning, problem-solving, and abstract thinking. It would be able to transfer knowledge from one domain to another, learn new tasks without human intervention, and adapt to new situations autonomously.

Artificial Superintelligence

A hypothetical form of AI that surpasses human intelligence and ability across a wide range of disciplines, including scientific creativity, general wisdom, and social skills. This type of AI would not only perform tasks better than humans but also make decisions and solve complex problems in ways that are currently beyond human comprehension. The development of artificial superintelligence raises significant ethical and existential questions, including the potential risks of losing control over such powerful systems and the impact on human society.

Core Components of AI Systems

AI systems are composed of several core components that enable their functionality:

Machine Learning (ML)

Machine learning (ML) is the backbone of most AI systems, where algorithms learn from and make predictions based on data. ML enables systems to improve their performance over time by identifying patterns and relationships within the data. It encompasses various techniques, including supervised learning, unsupervised learning, and reinforcement learning, each suited to distinct types of tasks and data structures.

Neural Networks

Neural networks are inspired by the human brain, these networks are a series of algorithms that capture relationships among data. They are particularly effective at processing patterns or trends within large sets of data. Neural networks, especially deep learning models, have revolutionized fields such as image and speech recognition, natural language processing, and game playing by enabling machines to perform complex tasks with high accuracy.

Robotics

The field of *robotics* integrates AI with mechanical and electronic systems to create physical entities that perform tasks autonomously or with minimal human intervention. Robotics leverages AI to enhance capabilities such as navigation, object manipulation, and interaction with environments, leading to advancements in areas like manufacturing, healthcare, and service industries. Autonomous drones, robotic surgical systems, and warehouse automation are prime examples.

Expert Systems

Expert systems are AI systems that mimic the decision-making ability of a human expert. By processing a set of rules, these systems provide conclusions, solutions, or diagnoses, applying reasoning capabilities and knowledge to a broad range of activities. Expert systems are widely used in medical diagnosis, financial forecasting, and customer support, where they enhance decision-making processes by offering expert-level insights and recommendations.

These components represent the foundational technologies that enable AI to act and react in a manner that closely resembles human intelligence, making them essential to the development and advancement of AI applications. They collectively contribute to the versatility and adaptability of AI systems, driving innovation across various sectors.

THE HISTORY OF AI

The history of AI is a fascinating journey that begins with the philosophical inquiries of ancient thinkers and stretches into the innovative advancements of today. Early musings about artificial beings can be traced back to Greek mythology, where mechanical men and intelligent machines were imagined. It was not until the twentieth century that the foundation for AI as understood today was laid. Philosophers and scientists began to explore the nature of human intelligence and pondered whether it could be replicated by machines. This intellectual curiosity set the stage for the development of AI, with pivotal moments like the introduction of formal logic and the birth of computer science.

One of the most significant milestones in the history of AI is the development of the Turing Test, proposed by British mathematician and logician Alan Turing in 1950. Turing's landmark paper, "Computing Machinery and Intelligence," posed the question, "Can machines think?" To answer this, Turing devised an experiment that has become a cornerstone in the field of AI. The Turing Test involves a human evaluator who interacts with both a machine and a human through a computer interface. If the evaluator cannot reliably distinguish between the machine and the human based on their responses, the machine is said to have demonstrated intelligent behavior indistinguishable from that of a human. This test was revolutionary in shifting the focus of AI from abstract philosophical debates to practical, testable criteria for machine intelligence.

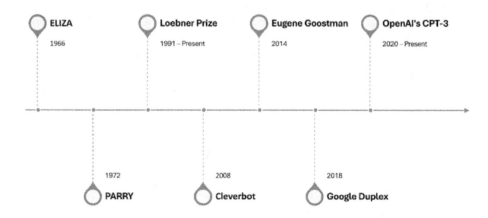

FIGURE 1.2 A timeline of significant milestones in the development and testing of AI systems.

Figure 1.2 is a timeline of significant milestones in the development and testing of AI systems in relation to the Turing Test. It begins with ELIZA in 1966, an early attempt at simulating human conversation, and progresses through notable advancements including PARRY in 1972, the Loebner Prize starting in 1991, Cleverbot in the early 2000s, Eugene Goostman in 2014, Google Duplex in 2018, and OpenAI's GPT-3 from 2020 onward. Each milestone marks a step forward in the ability of AI to generate human-like responses and engage in conversations that increasingly blur the lines between human and machine intelligence.

As AI research progressed, the 1950s and 1960s saw the creation of the first neural networks and the advent of symbolic AI, where researchers focused on creating systems that could manipulate symbols and perform logical reasoning. These early systems, though limited in scope and capability, laid the groundwork for more advanced AI developments. The field experienced various cycles of optimism and disappointment, often referred to as AI winters and summers, as researchers grappled with the complexities of replicating human cognition.

In the 1980s and 1990s, AI research expanded to include machine learning, a subset of AI that emphasizes the development of algorithms capable of learning from and making predictions based on data. This period also saw the rise of expert systems, which aimed to replicate the decision-making abilities of human experts. Despite the challenges and setbacks faced during this era, considerable progress was made, leading to a deeper understanding of both the potential and limitations of AI.

Modern AI has been propelled by significant advancements in computational power, the availability of vast datasets, and the development of sophisticated algorithms. Machine learning and deep learning, which involve training systems on substantial amounts of data to recognize patterns and make decisions, have been particularly transformative. AI is now embedded in many aspects of daily life, from virtual assistants and recommendation systems to autonomous vehicles and medical diagnostics. These developments highlight the continuous evolution of AI and its growing impact on technology and society.

The history of AI is marked by moments of inspiration, rigorous scientific inquiry, and groundbreaking technological achievements. By understanding the journey of AI from its philosophical roots to its present-day applications, insights into the potential future directions of this dynamic field are gained. This ongoing evolution reflects not only the technological advancements but also the changing societal attitudes and expectations toward intelligent systems.

EARLY CONCEPTS AND THEORIES

The conceptual groundwork for AI can be traced back to classical philosophers who speculated that human thought could be broken down into symbols and rules. This notion, later termed *symbolic AI*, posited that logical reasoning and problem-solving could be represented as formal systems, much like mathematics. Philosophers such as Aristotle and Descartes laid early theoretical foundations by exploring how logical processes might be systematically represented. Aristotle's work on syllogisms and deductive reasoning provided a framework for understanding logical inference, while Descartes' mechanistic view of the human body hinted at the possibility of replicating human functions with machines. These early ideas sowed the seeds for later scientific and technological advances, suggesting that human intelligence could be understood, modeled, and replicated by machines.

FIGURE 1.3 Two ornate pillars that symbolize the foundational principles set by ancient philosophers.

Figure 1.3 is an image of two ornate pillars that symbolize the foundational principles set by ancient philosophers that have contributed to the development of modern AI. Philosophers like Aristotle and Descartes laid the groundwork for logical reasoning and the mechanistic view of human thought. Their inquiries into the nature of intelligence, reasoning, and the human mind have influenced contemporary AI by providing the conceptual pillars for understanding and replicating human cognition through machines. These pillars represent the enduring legacy of ancient philosophical thought in the quest to create intelligent systems capable of emulating human-like reasoning and decision-making.

In the mid-twentieth century, these philosophical musings began to materialize into tangible innovations. Alan Turing, a pivotal figure in the history of computing, significantly contributed to this transition. In 1936, Turing introduced the concept of a universal machine capable of simulating any mathematical computation, a theoretical construct now known as the Turing Machine. This groundbreaking idea not only laid the foundation for modern computer science but also set the stage for the development of AI. Turing's later work, including his proposal of the Turing Test in 1950, further advanced the field by providing a practical framework for evaluating machine intelligence. His vision was instrumental in shifting the focus from purely theoretical discourse to empirical research and development, paving the way for the first computational machines and early AI systems.

The realization of these early concepts marked the beginning of a new era in which the abstract theories of symbolic reasoning began to be implemented in real-world applications. Researchers started building the first computers and exploring ways to enable these machines to perform tasks that would typically require human intelligence, such as solving puzzles and proving theorems. This period was characterized by a nascent optimism about the potential of AI, with pioneers like John McCarthy, Marvin Minsky, and Herbert Simon making significant contributions. McCarthy's invention of the Lisp programming language and the founding of the AI lab at MIT were pivotal in advancing AI research. The enthusiasm of this era set the stage for the remarkable advances that would follow in subsequent decades, including the development of more sophisticated algorithms, the advent of machine learning, and the integration of AI into various aspects of everyday life.

Key Milestones

The early development of AI was marked by several significant milestones that shaped the field's trajectory. In 1950, Alan Turing introduced the Turing Test, a groundbreaking method for evaluating a machine's ability to exhibit intelligent behavior equivalent to, or indistinguishable from, that of a human. This test laid the foundation for future AI research, challenging scientists to create systems capable of mimicking human cognitive functions. The Turing Test remains a touchstone in AI, symbolizing the quest to achieve human-like intelligence in machines.

The 1950s also witnessed the creation of the first neural networks, an attempt to simulate the human brain's interconnected neuron structure to process information. These early neural networks, though rudimentary, represented a significant step toward understanding and replicating the complexities of human cognition. Researchers like Frank Rosenblatt developed the Perceptron, a simple neural network model capable of learning from data. This model demonstrated the potential of machine learning and set the stage for more advanced neural network architectures.

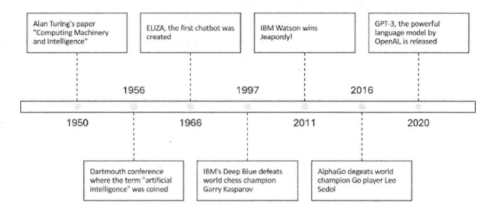

FIGURE 1.4 A timeline that highlights significant milestones in the history of AI.

Figure 1.4 is a timeline that highlights significant milestones in the history of AI. In 1950, Alan Turing published "Computing Machinery and Intelligence," proposing the Turing Test as a criterion of intelligence. The Dartmouth Conference in 1956 marked the formal birth of AI, coining the term "artificial intelligence." In 1966, ELIZA, the first chatbot, was created, simulating conversation by rephrasing user inputs. IBM's Deep Blue defeated world chess champion Garry Kasparov in 1997, highlighting AI's strategic thinking capabilities. In 2011, IBM's Watson won Jeopardy!, demonstrating advanced natural language processing. AlphaGo's victory over world champion Go player Lee Sedol in 2016 illustrated AI's prowess in mastering complex games. In 2020, OpenAI released GPT-3, a powerful language model that significantly advanced natural language understanding and generation. This timeline underscores the rapid evolution and expanding capabilities of AI technologies.

John McCarthy's development of the Lisp programming language in 1958 was another pivotal milestone. Lisp's powerful features, such as its support for symbolic computation and recursion, made it an ideal tool for developing AI algorithms and systems. McCarthy, often referred to as the father of AI, also organized the Dartmouth Conference in 1956, which officially marked the birth of AI as a field of study. This conference brought together leading researchers to discuss the potential of creating intelligent machines, setting the agenda for AI research for decades to come.

In the 1960s and 1970s, AI research made significant strides with the development of expert systems, which were designed to mimic the decision-making abilities of human experts. Programs like DENDRAL and MYCIN demonstrated the potential of AI in fields such as chemistry and medicine, providing early examples of how AI could be applied to solve complex real-world problems. The introduction of these expert systems highlighted the practical applications of AI and spurred further interest and investment in the field.

These early milestones set the stage for rapid advancements in AI. The combination of theoretical insights, such as those provided by the Turing Test, and practical tools like neural networks, Lisp, and expert systems, enabled researchers to explore new frontiers in machine learning and AI. This era of innovation laid the groundwork for the sophisticated AI technologies of today, from deep learning models to intelligent personal assistants. By understanding these key milestones, a deeper appreciation of the historical context and foundational principles that continue to drive AI research and development is gained.

Modern Developments

The resurgence of AI in the twenty-first century has been driven by exponential increases in computational power and the availability of vast amounts of data. These advancements have enabled significant innovations, such as deep learning, which mimics human brain functions by processing data through layers in neural networks. This technique has revolutionized fields like computer vision, natural language processing, and speech recognition, allowing AI systems to perform tasks with unprecedented accuracy and efficiency. Concurrently, big data analytics has empowered AI to analyze complex patterns and derive insights from massive datasets, facilitating advancements in areas ranging from healthcare diagnostics to financial forecasting.

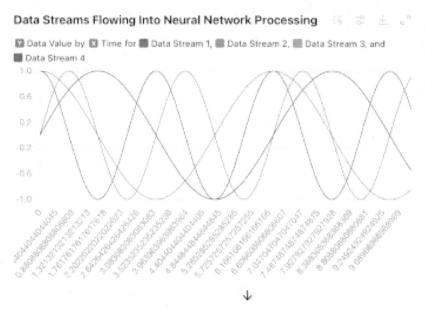

FIGURE 1.5 A visualization representing data streams being processed by a neural network.

Figure 1.5 is a visualization representing data streams being processed by a neural network. The chart depicts four data streams flowing into a highlighted section labeled "Neural Network Processing," symbolizing the transformation and analysis of large data sets in neural networks for big data analytics.

The development of AI frameworks and libraries, such as TensorFlow, PyTorch, and Keras, has further accelerated AI research and implementation by providing accessible tools for building and deploying sophisticated models. The introduction of specialized hardware, like GPUs and TPUs, has also optimized the training and inference processes for AI applications, making them faster and more efficient. Cloud computing platforms have made powerful AI resources accessible to smaller companies and individual developers, democratizing AI innovation.

As a result of these technological strides, AI has become deeply integrated into consumer technology and everyday life. Personal assistants like Siri, Alexa, and Google Assistant leverage AI to provide users with responsive, intelligent interactions. Recommendation systems on platforms such as Netflix, Amazon, and Spotify use AI algorithms to personalize content, enhancing user experiences. Moreover, AI's applications extend to autonomous vehicles, where it enables real-time decision-making and navigation. In healthcare, AI-driven diagnostic tools assist in early disease detection and personalized treatment plans. AI is also making strides in robotics, where it is used to create more adaptive and intelligent robotic systems for both industrial and domestic use. Financial services benefit from AI through fraud detection, credit scoring, and algorithmic trading.

These modern developments underscore the transformative potential of AI, highlighting its role in reshaping industries and improving the quality of life. As AI continues to evolve, its impact on society is expected to grow, opening new possibilities, and posing new challenges that will define the future of technology and human interaction. Ethical considerations, such as data privacy, bias in AI algorithms, and the future of work in an AI-driven economy, are becoming increasingly important topics of discussion as AI continues to advance. The ongoing research in explainable AI and the push for more transparent AI systems aim to address these concerns, ensuring that the benefits of AI are realized responsibly and equitably across society.

IMPORTANCE AND APPLICATIONS OF AI

AI is profoundly reshaping industries and everyday life, enhancing efficiency, innovation, and productivity across the board. This section examines the transformational impact of AI and provide a detailed look at its applications in key sectors such as healthcare, automotive, finance, and customer service, along with its ubiquitous presence in daily activities through smart home devices and personalized digital services.

Transformational Impact

AI is revolutionizing industries and society by driving unprecedented advancements in productivity, innovation, and efficiency. AI technologies are not just automating routine tasks but are also enhancing capabilities in data analysis and decision-making processes, thereby increasing the speed and quality of service across various sectors. This transformative impact is visible in everything from streamlined manufacturing processes to advanced research methodologies, boosting economic outputs and improving workplace dynamics.

Following are some sector-specific applications:

- healthcare
- automotive
- finance
- customer service

Healthcare

In the healthcare sector, AI is significantly improving outcomes by enhancing diagnostic accuracy, personalizing treatment plans, and even performing complex surgeries with robotic systems. Machine learning models can analyze medical images with greater precision than ever before, leading to early detection of conditions such as cancer. For instance, Google's DeepMind has developed algorithms capable of diagnosing eye diseases from retinal scans with accuracy comparable to that of expert ophthalmologists. Furthermore, AI-driven predictive analytics are being used to tailor treatment protocols to individual patients based on their unique genetic makeup. Companies like IBM Watson Health are using AI to analyze large datasets of clinical trials, medical journals, and patient records to provide personalized treatment recommendations. Robotic surgery systems, such as the da Vinci Surgical System, enable surgeons to perform delicate and complex procedures with enhanced precision and control, resulting in faster recovery times and reduced risk of complications.

Automotive

The automotive industry is leveraging AI to push the boundaries of autonomous vehicle technology and traffic management systems. AI algorithms process real-time data to enable self-driving cars to make split-second decisions about speed, routing, and safety. Companies like Tesla, Waymo, and Uber are at the forefront of developing self-driving cars that use AI to navigate complex urban environments, recognize traffic signals, and avoid obstacles. Additionally, AI is used in traffic management to optimize traffic flow, reduce congestion, and enhance road safety by analyzing traffic patterns and adjusting signals accordingly. For example, AI-powered traffic management systems in cities like Los Angeles and Pittsburgh use real-time data from traffic cameras and sensors to dynamically adjust traffic light timings, reducing travel time and emissions. AI is also being integrated into driver-assistance systems, such as adaptive cruise control and lane-keeping assist, to improve the safety and convenience of human-driven vehicles.

Finance

AI is transforming the finance sector by automating complex processes such as fraud detection, risk assessment, and algorithmic trading. AI systems analyze vast amounts of transaction data to identify fraudulent activities and alert banks before major losses occur. For example, companies like PayPal and Mastercard use machine learning models to detect unusual transaction patterns and prevent fraud. In trading, AI algorithms can execute trades at optimal prices, analyze market data for trends, and make high-frequency trades at a speed and volume beyond human capability. Hedge funds and investment firms like Renaissance Technologies and Two Sigma use AI to develop sophisticated trading strategies that capitalize on market inefficiencies. AI is also employed in credit scoring, where machine learning models assess the creditworthiness of loan applicants by analyzing a wide range of financial and nonfinancial data, thereby improving the accuracy and fairness of credit decisions.

Customer Service

AI-powered chatbots and virtual assistants are reshaping customer service, providing 24/7 support and personalized customer interactions. These AI systems can understand and process natural language to respond to customer inquiries, resolve issues, and even handle transactions, thereby improving the customer experience and reducing the workload on human staff. Companies like Amazon, with its Alexa, and Apple, with Siri, are using AI-driven virtual assistants to help customers with a wide range of tasks, from answering questions to making purchases. In addition, businesses are deploying AI chatbots on their Web sites and social media platforms to handle customer service requests. For example, the AI chatbot developed by Bank of America, known as Erica, assists customers with banking transactions, provides financial advice, and helps them manage their accounts. AI is also used to analyze customer feedback and sentiment, enabling companies to identify trends, improve their products and services, and provide a more personalized customer experience.

Daily Life

In daily life, AI's impact is becoming increasingly prevalent, transforming various aspects of routines and interactions with technology. Smart home devices, such as intelligent thermostats, lighting systems, and security cameras, utilize AI to learn user preferences and habits, creating a more comfortable, efficient, and secure living environment. These devices can adjust settings automatically, optimizing energy use and providing personalized comfort without the need for manual intervention. For instance, a smart thermostat can learn one's schedule and adjust the temperature to ensure their home is always at their preferred comfort level.

FIGURE 1.6 An illustration of a smart home environment where AI technologies enhance daily life.

Figure 1.6 is an illustration of a smart home environment where AI technologies enhance daily life. The scene highlights various AI-driven devices including personal assistants, smart appliances, and robotics, seamlessly interacting with family members. This visual represents the integration of AI in modern households, highlighting its role in improving convenience, efficiency, and connectivity within the home.

Moreover, AI-powered personal assistants like Amazon's Alexa, Google Assistant, and Apple's Siri have revolutionized how daily tasks are managed. These assistants can understand natural language commands, set reminders, send messages, make calls, and even control other smart devices in one's home. By predicting user needs and preferences, they streamline daily activities and enhance productivity. For example, they can provide weather updates, traffic reports, and news briefings tailored to one's interests, making their morning routine more efficient and informative.

AI's influence extends beyond the home, significantly altering how media is consumed and shopped. Recommendation algorithms on platforms like Netflix, Spotify, and YouTube analyze viewing and listening habits to suggest content that aligns with individual tastes. This personalized approach ensures that people discover new shows, movies, and music that they are likely to enjoy, enhancing their entertainment experience. Similarly, online retailers like Amazon use AI to provide personalized shopping suggestions based on one's browsing and purchase history, making it easier to find products that meet an individual's needs and preferences.

In addition to entertainment and shopping, AI also tailors news feeds and social media content. Algorithms on platforms like Facebook and Twitter analyze one's interactions to curate news stories and posts that are most relevant to them. This personalization can keep users informed about topics they care about, although it also raises concerns about filter bubbles and echo chambers, where one may be exposed to a narrower range of viewpoints.

Overall, AI's integration into daily life is reshaping how technology is interacted with, making environments more responsive and personalized. As AI continues to evolve, its presence in everyday activities is likely to grow, offering even more sophisticated and intuitive ways to enhance daily experiences.

ETHICAL CONSIDERATIONS

As AI continues to advance, it raises profound ethical questions and challenges that must be addressed to ensure its development benefits all of society. This section examines the ethical considerations of AI, including the implications of autonomy in machines, the risks of bias and fairness in AI systems, the privacy concerns associated with AI technologies, and the critical need for robust regulation and governance to guide responsible AI development and deployment.

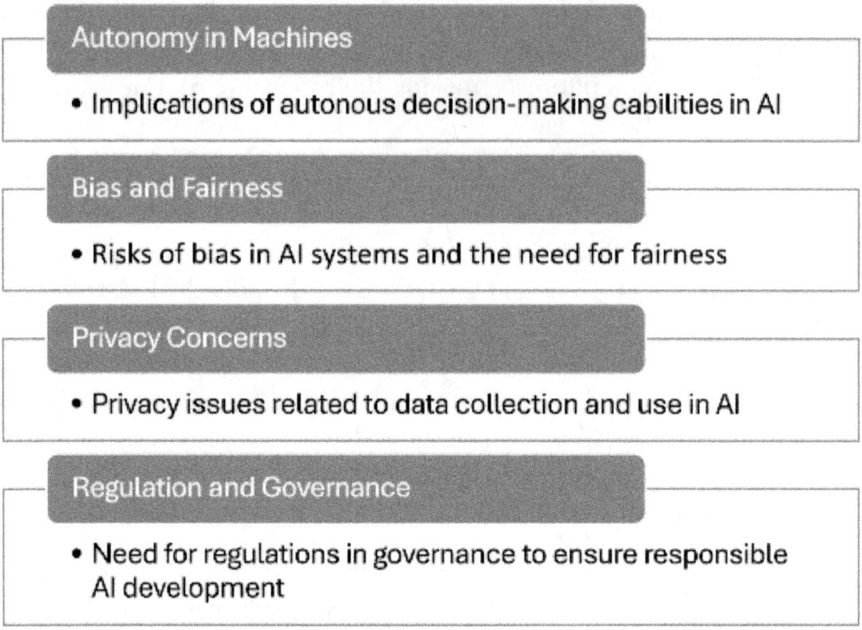

FIGURE 1.7 A diagram that outlines four key areas of ethical considerations in AI.

Figure 1.7 is a diagram outlines four key areas of ethical considerations in AI: autonomy in machines, bias and fairness, privacy concerns, and regulation and governance. It highlights the importance of addressing these issues to ensure responsible and beneficial AI development and deployment.

Fundamental Questions

The development of AI poses significant ethical challenges, particularly concerning the creation and deployment of autonomous systems. These machines can make decisions that impact human lives, such as in autonomous vehicles and medical diagnostics. There is a critical need to consider how these decisions are made, the accountability for outcomes, and the moral implications of transferring decision-making from humans to machines. For example, in the case of autonomous vehicles, ethical dilemmas arise in scenarios where the vehicle must choose between different harmful outcomes. Additionally, questions also arise about the potential loss of jobs due to automation and the broader societal impacts this could have. The displacement of workers by AI technologies could exacerbate economic inequalities and necessitate policies for reskilling and supporting affected individuals.

Bias and Fairness

AI systems often reflect the biases present in their training data or the subjective decisions of their designers, which can lead to unfair outcomes when deployed. For instance, facial recognition technologies have shown differing levels of accuracy across different racial groups, raising concerns about systemic bias. An example is the misidentification of individuals of certain ethnicities, leading to wrongful arrests or surveillance. It is crucial to implement methodologies that detect and mitigate biases and to develop AI technologies that promote fairness and equity. This involves diverse and representative data collection, transparency in algorithmic decision-making, and ongoing monitoring of outcomes. Researchers and developers must be vigilant about the sources of bias in data and design processes, ensuring that AI applications do not perpetuate or amplify existing societal biases.

Privacy

Privacy concerns in AI center around the extensive data AI systems require, including personal and sensitive information. The storage, use, and potential misuse of such data pose significant privacy risks. For example, AI applications in healthcare might use personal health data to improve diagnostics, but if not effectively managed, this data could be exposed to unauthorized parties. Effective measures must be implemented to ensure data protection, such as data anonymization, secure data storage practices, and strict adherence to privacy regulations like the General Data Protection Regulation (GDPR) in Europe. Additionally, users should have control over their data and understand how it is used by AI systems. Clear consent mechanisms and the ability to opt-out are essential for maintaining trust in AI technologies.

Regulation and Governance

The rapid development and deployment of AI technologies necessitate robust regulatory frameworks to ensure they are used responsibly. This includes establishing clear guidelines for ethical AI development, accountability standards for AI decisions, and protections against misuse. Governments and international bodies are called to play a significant role in crafting these regulations to manage the societal and ethical implications of AI. Effective governance should also involve stakeholders from various sectors to ensure that AI technologies benefit all parts of society without exacerbating inequalities or harming vulnerable groups. For instance, the European Commission has proposed the Artificial Intelligence Act, which aims to regulate high-risk AI applications and ensure they adhere to ethical standards. Collaboration between policymakers, industry leaders, and civil society is essential to create a balanced and inclusive regulatory environment.

AI APPLICATION: CREATE A SIMPLE RULE-BASED CHATBOT

In this AI Application, users will build a simple rule-based chatbot using Python. This chatbot will respond to basic user queries using predefined rules. This guide provides step-by-step instructions to help readers follow along easily.

- *Step 1*: Set up the development environment.

- *Step 2*: Create the chatbot script.

- *Step 3*: Run the chatbot.

- *Step 4*: Understand the script.

Step 1: Set Up the Development Environment

1. Install Python

   - Follow the instructions in the previous example to download and install Python if that has not been done already.

2. Install Necessary Libraries

   - Open a terminal or command prompt.

   - Install the *"nltk"* library, which is useful for natural language processing tasks, by typing:

   pip install nltk

Step 2: Create the Chatbot Script

1. Open your code editor.

   - Use preferred text editor or IDE (e.g., Visual Studio Code, PyCharm, or even a plain text editor).

2. Create a new Python file.

   - Create a new file named *"chatbot.py"*.

3. Import necessary libraries.

   - At the top of the *"chatbot.py"* file, import the necessary libraries:

```
1   import nltk
2   from nltk.chat.util import Chat, reflections
```

4. Define Predefined Responses

   - Create a list of predefined patterns and responses for the chatbot to use.

```
3   pairs = [
4       [
5       r"my name is (.*)",
6       ["Hello %1, how can I help you today?",]
7       ],
8       [
9       r"hi|hey|hello",
10      ["Hello! How can I assist you?",]
11      ],
12      [
13      r"what is your name?",
14      ["I am a chatbot created to help you with your queries
15      ],
16      [
17      r"how are you?",
18      ["I am just a program, but I'm here to assist you!",]
19      ],
20      [
21      r"quit",
22      ["Goodbye! Have a nice day.",]
23      ],
24      ]
```

5. Create the chatbot.

   • Initialize the chatbot using the predefined patterns and responses:

```
25  def chatbot():
26      print("Hi, I am a chatbot. Type 'quit' to exit.")
27  chat = Chat(pairs, reflections)
28  chat.converse()
29  if __name__ == "__main__":
30      chatbot()
```

Step 3: Run the Chatbot

1. Run the script.
   a. Open a terminal or command prompt.
   b. Navigate to the directory where the *"chatbot.py"* file is located.
   c. Run the script by typing:
      python chatbot.py
2. Interact with the Chatbot

   a. A prompt should appear in the terminal:

   > Hi, I am a chatbot. Type 'quit' to exit.

   b. Try typing different inputs to see how the chatbot responds. For example:

   > User: hi
   > Chatbot: Hello! How can I assist you?
   >
   > User: my name is John
   > Chatbot: Hello John, how can I help you today?
   >
   > User: what is your name?
   > Chatbot: I am a chatbot created to help you with your queries.
   >
   > User: quit
   > Chatbot: Goodbye! Have a wonderful day.

Step 4: Understand the Script

- *Imports*: The script imports necessary functions from the *"nltk"* library.

- *Patterns and Responses*: A list of tuples ("pairs") is defined, where each tuple contains a regex pattern and corresponding responses.

- *Chatbot Function*: The *"chatbot"* function initializes the chatbot with the predefined patterns and starts a conversation.

- *Main Block*: The script checks if it is run as the main module and calls the "chatbot" function.

```
1   import nltk
2   from nltk.chat.util import Chat, reflections
3   pairs = [
4       [
5       r"my name is (.*)",
6       ["Hello %1, how can I help you today?",]
7       ],
8       [
9       r"hi|hey|hello",
10      ["Hello! How can I assist you?",]
11      ],
12      [
13      r"what is your name?",
14      ["I am a chatbot created to help you with your queries
15      ],
16      [
17      r"how are you?",
18      ["I am just a program, but I'm here to assist you!",]
19      ],
20      [
21      r"quit",
22      ["Goodbye! Have a nice day.",]
23      ],
24      ]
25  def chatbot():
26      print("Hi, I am a chatbot. Type 'quit' to exit.")
27  chat = Chat(pairs, reflections)
28  chat.converse()
29  if __name__ == "__main__":
30      chatbot()
```

Following these steps enables users to successfully create a simple rule-based chatbot that can respond to basic user queries using predefined rules. This exercise provides a foundational understanding of how chatbots work, setting the stage for more complex AI projects as readers progress through the book.

CONCLUSION

This opening chapter traversed the expansive landscape of AI, setting the stage for a deeper understanding of this transformative technology. It began by defining AI, establishing a foundational understanding of its capabilities and various forms. AI encompasses a broad range of tasks that mimic human intelligence, from decision-making and visual perception to speech recognition and language translation. Exploring these fundamental aspects laid the groundwork for appreciating the complexity and potential of AI technologies.

The rich history of AI was explored, tracing its origins from the philosophical inquiries of ancient thinkers to the sophisticated AI systems of today. Key milestones, such as the introduction of the Turing Test and the development of neural networks, have been pivotal in shaping the field. These historical insights highlight the continuous evolution of AI and underscore its growing impact on modern society. Moreover, core components of AI, including machine learning, neural networks, robotics, and expert systems, were examined, revealing how they collectively drive the functionality and advancement of AI applications.

Distinct types of AI were discussed, distinguishing between narrow AI, general AI, and artificial superintelligence. Understanding these distinctions is crucial for grasping the current capabilities and future potential of AI. Narrow AI excels in specific tasks, general AI aims to replicate human intelligence broadly, and artificial superintelligence represents a theoretical leap beyond human capabilities. These categories provide a framework for discussing the diverse applications and implications of AI.

Modern developments in AI were also examined, driven by significant advancements in computational power and data availability. Innovations such as deep learning and big data analytics have revolutionized various fields, from healthcare and finance to automotive and customer service. AI's integration into daily life, through smart home devices and personalized digital services, demonstrates its pervasive influence and the profound changes it brings to our routines and interactions with technology.

Ethical considerations arising with the development and deployment of AI were highlighted, including concerns about autonomy, bias, privacy, and the need for robust regulation and governance. Addressing these ethical challenges is essential to ensure that AI technologies are developed and used responsibly, benefiting all of society without exacerbating inequalities or causing harm.

As the journey continues into subsequent chapters, this foundational knowledge will be built upon, examining specific AI technologies, applications, and ethical issues more deeply. This comprehensive introduction provides the necessary context for a thorough exploration of the multifaceted world of AI. By understanding the principles and history of AI, readers are better equipped to engage with its present realities and future possibilities, recognizing both its potential and the responsibilities it entails.

## CHAPTER 2

FOUNDATIONS OF MACHINE LEARNING

Machine learning (ML) is the backbone of many AI systems, providing the statistical framework for computers to learn from data. This chapter introduces the core concepts of ML, including supervised and unsupervised learning methods, and the processes of model evaluation and selection. Through detailed explanations and examples, readers will examine how these techniques enable machines to make predictions and decisions, transforming raw data into actionable insights. This foundational knowledge is crucial for anyone looking to understand or work in the field of AI.

INTRODUCTION TO MACHINE LEARNING

Machine learning (ML) is a fundamental pillar of artificial intelligence (AI), revolutionizing the way computers learn from and interact with data. At its core, ML involves creating algorithms that enable computers to learn from experience, adapt to the latest information, and make decisions based on data. This self-improving capability distinguishes ML from traditional programming, where specific instructions are required for each task. By analyzing vast amounts of data, ML models identify patterns and insights that allow them to perform tasks such as recognizing images, understanding speech, and predicting future trends with remarkable accuracy.

Understanding the basic principles and components of ML is crucial for grasping its potential and applications. ML systems typically involve data collection, data preparation, model selection, training, evaluation, and optimization. Key components include algorithms that process data, datasets that provide information, features that represent data characteristics, models that learn from data, loss functions that measure prediction accuracy, and optimization algorithms that refine model performance. These elements work together to create powerful systems capable of tackling complex problems across various domains. This foundational knowledge sets the stage for exploring the distinct types of ML, including supervised, unsupervised, and reinforcement learning, and their diverse applications in fields such as healthcare, finance, and transportation.

Definition and Scope

ML is a specialized subset of AI that empowers systems to automatically learn and improve from experience without being explicitly programmed. This capability distinguishes ML from traditional programming, where tasks are performed based on predefined rules and explicit instructions guide data processing. In ML, algorithms analyze and process vast amounts of data, identify patterns, and generate rules based on these patterns. This enables the system to make predictions, classify information, and provide insights dynamically, adjusting its outputs as it encounters new data.

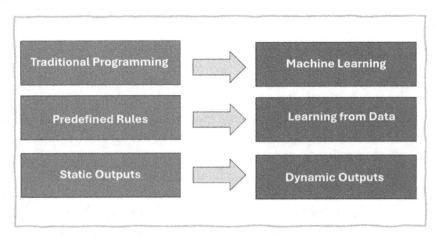

FIGURE 2.1 Traditional programming versus machine learning.

Figure 2.1 contrasts traditional programming with ML, highlighting key differences between the two approaches. The left side shows "Traditional Programming" leading to "Predefined Rules" and "Static

Outputs," representing a static approach based on explicit instructions. The right side displays "Machine Learning," which involves "Learning from Data" and results in "Dynamic Outputs," highlighting a flexible approach where systems adapt based on data analysis. Green arrows between the components emphasize the transition from traditional programming to ML, underscoring the shift from static, rule-based systems to dynamic, data-driven ones. The border around the figure adds a visual emphasis to the comparison.

The scope of ML is broad, encompassing various techniques and approaches to achieve its learning capabilities. Supervised learning involves training models on labeled data, where the correct output is known, to predict outcomes for new, unseen data. Unsupervised learning deals with unlabeled data and aims to uncover hidden patterns or intrinsic structures within the data. Reinforcement learning involves an agent interacting with an environment, learning to make decisions through trial and error, and receiving feedback in the form of rewards or penalties. These distinct types of ML enable applications across diverse fields, such as healthcare, finance, marketing, and autonomous systems, demonstrating the transformative potential of ML in addressing complex real-world challenges.

How ML Works

ML algorithms employ sophisticated statistical methods to identify patterns and insights within data. The process begins with the training phase, where these algorithms are exposed to large datasets. During training, the algorithms iteratively adjust and refine their parameters by minimizing errors through a process known as optimization. This involves techniques such as gradient descent, where the algorithm continuously updates its parameters to reduce the difference between predicted and actual outcomes. Over time, this iterative process enhances the accuracy and predictive power of the model, allowing it to make more precise and reliable decisions.

One of the key advantages of ML is its ability to adapt without requiring manual intervention beyond the initial programming. Once the algorithms are set in motion, they learn autonomously by analyzing the statistical properties of the data they process. This self-improving capability means that as more data is fed into the system, the algorithms become increasingly adept at recognizing patterns and making predictions. This dynamic adaptability is what sets ML apart from traditional programming, enabling it to handle complex and evolving data scenarios with greater efficiency and effectiveness.

Key Components

The fundamental elements of any ML system include:

Data

The raw input that feeds into the model, which can be in various forms such as numbers, words, images, and so on. This data is typically divided into training and testing sets. The training set is used to teach the model, while the testing set is used to evaluate its performance.

Model

The framework or architecture that makes predictions or decisions based on input data. Models vary widely depending on the specific ML task—such as regression, classification, or clustering. For example, linear regression models predict continuous outcomes, while classification models like decision trees or support vector machines (SVMs) categorize data into discrete classes.

Learning Algorithm

The method by which the model is trained from the data. This includes a variety of algorithms like decision trees, neural networks, and gradient boosting, among others. Each algorithm has its own strengths and weaknesses, making them suitable for distinct types of tasks.

Evaluation Metrics

Criteria used to assess the performance of the model. Common metrics include accuracy, precision, recall, and the area under the curve (AUC) for classification tasks and mean squared error (MSE) or mean absolute error (MAE) for regression tasks. These metrics help determine how well the model generalizes to new, unseen data and guides further tuning and improvement.

By understanding these key components and how they interact, readers can appreciate the complex yet powerful nature of ML and its potential to solve diverse and intricate problems.

SUPERVISED LEARNING

Supervised learning is a powerful method in ML where models are trained using labeled data. This section explores key algorithms and their practical applications, illustrating how this method enables predictive accuracy across diverse scenarios.

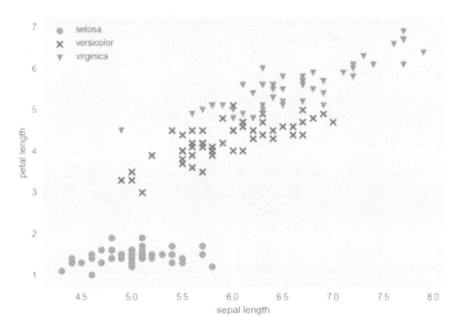

FIGURE 2.2 A scatter plot that illustrates a supervised learning example.

Figure 2.2 is a scatter plot that illustrates a supervised learning example using the Iris dataset to classify three distinct species of the Iris flower: setosa, versicolor, and virginica. The x-axis represents the sepal length, while the y-axis represents the petal length. Each species is distinguished by a different marker and color: red circles for setosa, blue crosses for versicolor, and green triangles for virginica. This plot shows the labeled training data used to train a ML model. The clear separation of setosa from the other two species highlights its distinct morphological characteristics, while versicolor and virginica show some overlap, indicating closer similarities in their sepal and petal lengths. This visualization demonstrates how labeled data can be used to train models to predict the species of Iris flowers based on their sepal and petal measurements.

Concept and Mechanism

Supervised learning is a predominant method in ML where a model is trained using a labeled dataset. Each data point in this dataset includes an input paired with a correct output (label), allowing the model to learn a function that can predict the output associated with new inputs. This method relies on using these known pairs to adjust the model parameters until it can accurately map inputs to outputs, a process often referred to as "learning from examples."

Common Algorithms

Several key algorithms dominate the field of supervised learning, each suitable for distinct types of data and problems:

Linear Regression

Used for predicting continuous outcomes, linear regression fits a line to data points to model the relationship between input variables and a continuous output variable.

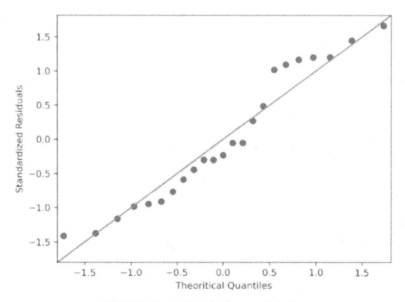

FIGURE 2.3 A Q-Q (quantile-quantile) plot.

Figure 2.3 is a Q-Q (quantile-quantile) plot, which compares the standardized residuals of a dataset against the theoretical quantiles of a normal distribution. The blue dots represent the observed data points, while the red line represents the expected distribution if the data were perfectly normally distributed. Deviations of the points from the red line indicate departures from normality. This plot is used to assess whether the residuals follow a normal distribution, which is a common assumption in many statistical models.

Logistic Regression

Despite its name, logistic regression is used for binary classification tasks, not regression. It estimates the probabilities of binary outcomes based on input features, using a logistic function.

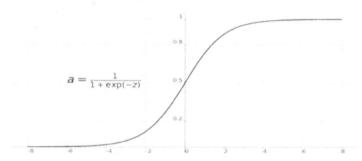

FIGURE 2.4 An illustration of the sigmoid function.

Figure 2.4 illustrates the sigmoid function, a common activation function used in neural networks. The sigmoid function is defined as $a = \frac{1}{1+e^{-z}}$, where z is the input value. The plot shows how the sigmoid function maps any input value z to an output value a in the range (0, 1). The S-shaped curve of the sigmoid function demonstrates its capability to smoothly transition between the output values, making it useful for models that need to predict probabilities.

Decision Trees

This algorithm models decisions and their consequences as a tree, including chance event outcomes, resource costs, and utility. It is a straightforward way of visualizing decisions and is particularly useful for classification and regression.

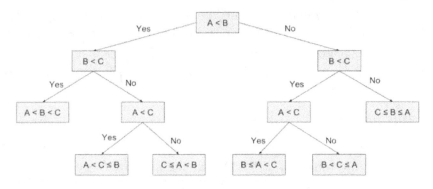

FIGURE 2.5 A decision tree.

Figure 2.5 depicts a decision tree, which is a fundamental tool used in ML for classification and regression tasks. The tree starts with a root node that asks the question $A<BA<B$. Depending on the answer (Yes or No), the tree branches out to subsequent nodes, each posing another question based on comparisons among variables AA, BB, and CC. The leaf nodes at the end of each branch provide the final classification or decision outcome. Decision trees are valuable for their simplicity and interpretability in making data-driven decisions.

Support Vector Machines (SVMs)

SVMs are powerful for classification tasks, especially in high-dimensional spaces. They work by finding the hyperplane that best separates different classes in the feature space, maximizing the margin between different class data points.

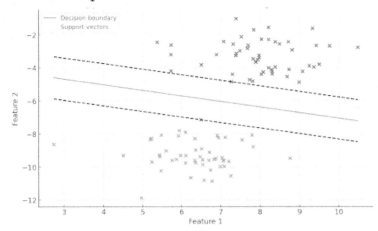

FIGURE 2.6 The concept of an SVM.

Figure 2.6 illustrates the concept of an SVM for binary classification. The plot shows two classes of data points, represented by blue and green dots, which are separated by a hyperplane. The SVM algorithm identifies the optimal hyperplane (red line) that maximizes the margin between the two classes. The margin is defined by the distance to the nearest data points from either class, which are called support vectors (highlighted as larger blue and green dots). The dashed lines represent the boundaries of the margin. The SVM aims to maximize this margin to ensure the best separation between the classes.

Applications

Supervised learning has a broad array of practical applications across various domains, some of which are described in the following sections.

Spam Detection

Email services use supervised learning to classify emails as spam or not spam by learning from features such as sender details, subject line, and email content. For instance, Google's Gmail employs ML algorithms that analyze millions of emails to identify patterns and characteristics common in spam, helping to filter out unwanted messages effectively.

Sentiment Analysis

Companies analyze reviews and social media posts using supervised learning to determine the sentiment expressed in the text, helping in brand monitoring and product development. For example, businesses like Amazon and Netflix use sentiment analysis to gauge customer satisfaction and refine their products and services based on feedback, enhancing user experience and engagement.

Credit Scoring Systems

Financial institutions employ supervised learning to assess the creditworthiness of borrowers by analyzing past financial data and repayment histories to predict future default probabilities. Companies like FICO use advanced ML models to evaluate numerous financial factors, ensuring more accurate and fair credit scoring, which benefits both lenders and borrowers by providing better risk assessments.

Medical Diagnosis

Supervised learning models assist in diagnosing diseases by analyzing medical records and imaging data. For instance, AI systems can learn to identify early signs of conditions like diabetic retinopathy from retinal images, enabling early intervention and treatment, which improves patient outcomes.

Fraud Detection

Banks and payment processors use supervised learning to detect fraudulent transactions. By training models on historical transaction data, these systems can identify unusual patterns that suggest fraud, allowing for real-time alerts and prevention measures, thereby protecting customers and financial institutions from significant losses.

Predictive Maintenance

Manufacturing and utility companies implement supervised learning to predict equipment failures before they occur. By analyzing sensor data and historical maintenance records, these models can forecast when a machine is likely to fail, enabling preemptive repairs and minimizing downtime, which enhances operational efficiency and reduces costs.

Customer Churn Prediction

Businesses use supervised learning to predict which customers are likely to leave their service based on historical behavior and engagement data. Telecom companies, for instance, analyze call patterns, service usage, and support interactions to identify at-risk customers and implement retention strategies to keep them engaged.

Stock Market Prediction

Investors and financial analysts use supervised learning models to predict stock price movements by analyzing historical price data, trading volumes, and other relevant financial indicators. These predictions help in making informed trading decisions, improving investment strategies, and maximizing returns.

By leveraging supervised learning, organizations can optimize processes, improve decision-making, and enhance customer experiences across various sectors, demonstrating the transformative potential of ML technologies.

UNSUPERVISED LEARNING

Unsupervised learning allows algorithms to identify patterns and relationships in data without the guidance of labeled outcomes. This section will help readers establish and understand the mechanisms and uses of unsupervised learning techniques, highlighting their ability to discover hidden structures in complex datasets.

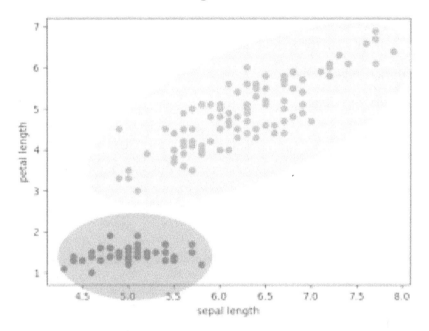

FIGURE 2.7 An example of unsupervised learning.

Figure 2.7 is an example of unsupervised learning using the Iris dataset. Here, the data points represent measurements of sepal length and petal length, with each point corresponding to an individual Iris flower. Unlike supervised learning, the data points are not labeled with specific species. Instead, the unsupervised learning algorithm, a clustering algorithm such as k-means, has grouped the data into two clusters based on their similarities. The clusters are visually highlighted with different colored ellipses: a blue ellipse for one cluster and a yellow ellipse for the other. This clustering reveals natural groupings within the data, indicating that the algorithm has identified patterns without prior knowledge of the species labels. This method helps in discovering underlying structures in the data, which can then be used for further analysis or labeling.

Concept and Mechanism

Unsupervised learning is a branch of ML that operates on data without predefined labels, allowing the system to identify patterns and structures on its own. This approach is key in scenarios where the data lacks annotations or where the interest lies in discovering hidden relationships and patterns within the data set itself. Unsupervised learning algorithms organize data into clusters or groups based on similarities, detect anomalies that deviate from the norm, or reduce the dimensionality of data for analysis simplification.

Common Algorithms

Clustering Algorithms

Clustering is a common unsupervised learning technique used to group sets of objects into clusters that are meaningful, useful, or both. The k-means clustering algorithm partitions data into K distinct, nonoverlapping clusters based on their features, minimizing variance within each cluster. *Hierarchical clustering* builds a tree of clusters and does not require a preset number of clusters.

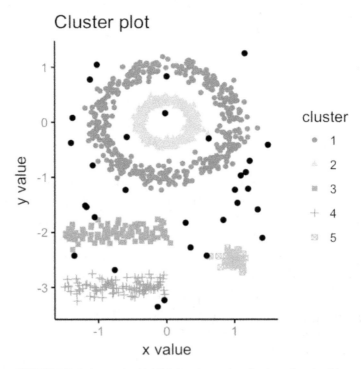

FIGURE 2.8 A cluster plot highlighting the results of a clustering algorithm.

Figure 2.8 depicts a cluster plot highlighting the results of a clustering algorithm applied to a dataset. The plot displays five distinct clusters, each represented by different markers and colors. Cluster 1 (blue dots) forms a large outer ring, while Cluster 2 (yellow triangles) forms a smaller inner ring. Cluster 3 (grey squares) and Cluster 4 (red plus signs) are linearly separated clusters located toward the bottom of the plot. Cluster 5 (light blue squares) is a smaller cluster located on the right side. The black dots represent outliers or data points that do not belong to any of the identified clusters. This visualization demonstrates how clustering techniques can segment data into distinct groups based on their features.

Association Algorithms

These algorithms are used to find relationships between variables in large databases. The Apriori algorithm identifies frequent item sets in transactional data and is widely used for market basket analysis. Eclat algorithm, like Apriori, uses a depth-first search technique to compute frequent item sets, often performing faster by reducing computational overhead.

FIGURE 2.9 A network graph.

Figure 2.9 illustrates a network graph, which is commonly used to represent relationships and connections between various entities in a dataset. Each node (green circle) represents an individual entity, while the edges (lines) connecting the nodes indicate relationships or interactions between these entities. The yellow nodes are central points that connect to multiple clusters of nodes, highlighting important hubs within the network. This visualization helps in understanding the structure of the network, identifying clusters, and analyzing the centrality and connectivity of different entities. It is a powerful tool for uncovering patterns and insights in complex datasets, especially in fields like social network analysis, biology, and information science.

Dimensionality Reduction Techniques

Techniques like principal component analysis (PCA) and t-distributed stochastic neighbor embedding (t-SNE) are crucial for reducing the number of variables under consideration. PCA transforms a large set of variables into a smaller one that still contains most of the information in large datasets. t-SNE, particularly useful in visualizing high-dimensional data, helps interpret the structure of data by reducing dimensions and allowing for plotting in a two or three-dimensional space.

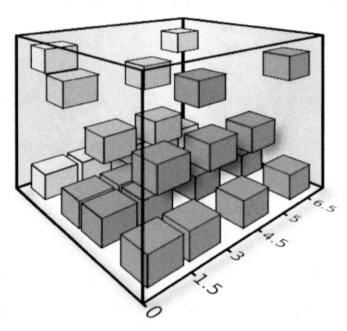

FIGURE 2.10 A 3D scatter plot using colored cubes to represent data points in a three-dimensional space.

Figure 2.10 depicts a 3D scatter plot using colored cubes to represent data points in a three-dimensional space. Each cube's position is determined by three variables plotted along the x, y, and z axes, while distinct colors indicate distinct categories or clusters within the dataset. This type of visualization is particularly useful for exploring relationships and patterns in high-dimensional data, allowing for a more intuitive understanding of how data points are distributed and how they relate to each other across multiple dimensions. It is commonly used in fields such as data science, ML, and multivariate analysis to reveal insights that might not be apparent in lower dimensional representations.

Applications

Customer Segmentation

Unsupervised learning can analyze customer data and segment customers into groups with similar behaviors for targeted marketing, enhancing customer service and retention strategies. For example, e-commerce platforms like Amazon and fashion retailers like Zara use clustering algorithms to group customers based on purchasing habits, browsing behavior, and demographic information. These segments help businesses tailor marketing campaigns, personalize recommendations, and create more effective loyalty programs, boosting customer satisfaction and retention.

Market Basket Analysis

Retailers use unsupervised learning to analyze purchase patterns, discovering items frequently bought together and using this information for cross-selling strategies or store layout optimizations. For instance, grocery stores use association rule learning to identify products that are often purchased together, such as bread and butter. This insight helps them place related items near each other in stores, design promotional offers, and optimize inventory management, thereby increasing sales and improving the shopping experience.

Anomaly Detection

In various industries, from banking to manufacturing, unsupervised learning algorithms detect unusual patterns or anomalies that could indicate fraudulent activity or potential failures in machinery, often leading to significant cost savings and increased security. Banks like JPMorgan Chase use anomaly detection to monitor transaction data for signs of fraud, quickly identifying and mitigating suspicious activities. Similarly, manufacturers like General Electric use these algorithms to analyze sensor data from machinery, detecting early signs of mechanical failures and scheduling preventive maintenance, which reduces downtime and maintenance costs.

Social Network Analysis

Unsupervised learning is used to analyze the structure of social networks, identifying influential users, community clusters, and patterns of interaction. Platforms like Facebook and LinkedIn utilize graph-based clustering techniques to understand user connections and interactions, which helps in recommending new connections, optimizing content delivery, and improving user engagement.

Document Clustering

Organizations employ unsupervised learning to automatically organize large collections of documents into meaningful clusters. For instance, news agencies like Reuters use clustering algorithms to group articles by topics, making it easier to manage and retrieve information. This technique is also applied in legal and academic fields to categorize vast amounts of text data, enhancing searchability and knowledge discovery.

Image Compression

In the field of computer vision, unsupervised learning algorithms are used for image compression by identifying patterns and redundancies in pixel data. Techniques like PCA and K-means clustering reduce the dimensionality of image data, enabling more efficient storage and transmission without significant loss of quality. Companies like Google use these methods to optimize image storage and retrieval in their services.

Bioinformatics

Researchers use unsupervised learning to analyze biological data, such as gene expression profiles, to identify patterns and relationships that might indicate disease markers or genetic predispositions. This analysis helps in understanding complex biological processes and developing personalized medicine strategies. For example, clustering algorithms can group patients with similar genetic profiles to tailor specific treatments and improve healthcare outcomes.

By leveraging the power of unsupervised learning, businesses and researchers can uncover hidden patterns and insights in data, driving innovation and efficiency across various domains.

MODEL EVALUATION AND SELECTION

Evaluating and selecting the right model is crucial for achieving reliable and effective ML outcomes. This section covers the essential metrics and validation techniques used to assess model performance, ensuring the selection of the most suitable model for specific tasks.

Evaluation Metrics

When assessing ML models, several metrics are employed to measure their performance accurately. Accuracy measures the overall correctness of the model across all predictions, making it suitable for balanced classification problems. It is important to not that in scenarios where the data is imbalanced, accuracy may not be sufficient.

Precision and Recall

Precision and recall are particularly useful in contexts where false positives and false negatives carry different costs. *Precision* measures the accuracy of positive predictions (i.e., the number of true positives divided by the number of true positives and false positives). *Recall* measures the model's ability to identify all actual positives (i.e., the number of true positives divided by the number of true positives and false negatives).

The F1 Score

The harmonic mean of precision and recall, providing a single metric that balances both concerns, especially in unbalanced datasets. This makes it particularly useful when the cost of false positives and false negatives is equally important.

Mean Squared Error (MSE) and Root Mean Squared Error (RMSE)

For regression models, metrics such as mean squared error (MSE) and root mean squared Error (RMSE) are critical. MSE is the average of the squares of the errors—the average squared difference between the estimated values and the actual value. RMSE is the square root of MSE, which scales the error back to the original units of the output, making interpretation straightforward. These metrics are essential in determining how well the model predicts continuous outcomes.

Area Under the Receiver Operating Characteristic Curve (AUC-ROC)

Another important metric, particularly for binary classification problems. It measures the ability of the model to distinguish between the classes across all threshold values. AUC-ROC provides insight into the model's performance by evaluating the trade-off between true positive rate and false positive rate.

Validation Techniques

Ensuring that a ML model performs well on unseen data is crucial for its reliability and utility. *Train-test split* is a basic approach where the data is divided into two sets: one for training and the other for testing, allowing evaluation on clean, unseen data.

Cross-Validation

Cross-validation (particularly k-fold cross-validation) enhances this process by cycling through multiple splits of the data into training and testing sets. In k-fold cross-validation, the data is divided into k subsets, and the model is trained and tested k times, each time using a different subset as the test set and the remaining as the training set. This provides a more robust estimate of the model's performance on new data, reducing the risk of overfitting.

Bootstrapping

Another technique, especially useful in estimating the uncertainty of a model's predictions by resampling the training set with replacement and training new models on these samples. This method helps in understanding how changes in the training data affect the predictions, which is vital for models deployed in dynamic real-world environments.

Model Selection

The process of model selection involves choosing the best model based on its performance metrics and validation results. This decision is influenced by a trade-off between model complexity and generalizability. More complex models, such as deep neural networks, may perform better on the training data but can overfit, meaning they perform poorly on new, unseen data. Conversely, simpler models might underfit, failing to capture important nuances in the data.

Techniques like the *Akaike information criterion (AIC)* or *Bayesian information criterion (BIC)* can help in model selection by penalizing excessive complexity. These criteria balance model fit and complexity by adding a penalty term for the number of parameters, discouraging overfitting.

The chosen model should balance accuracy with the ability to generalize from training data to real-world applications, ensuring it performs well under varied conditions. This balance is crucial for developing robust, reliable ML systems that can adapt to new data and continue to deliver valuable insights and predictions.

AI APPLICATION: IMPLEMENT A LINEAR REGRESSION MODEL TO PREDICT HOUSE PRICES

In this AI application, readers will implement a linear regression model to predict house prices using Python, Pandas, and Scikit-learn. This guide provides step-by-step instructions for data preprocessing, model training, and evaluation:

- *Step 1*: Set Up the Development Environment

- *Step 2*: Prepare the Dataset

- *Step 3*: Implement the Linear Regression Model

- *Step 4*: Run the Script

Step 1: Set Up the Development Environment

1. Install Python

    - Follow the instructions in the previous examples to download and install Python.

2. Install Necessary Libraries

    - Open a terminal or command prompt.

    - Install the required libraries by typing:

        pip install pandas scikit-learn matplotlib

Step 2: Prepare the Dataset

1. Create a Sample Dataset

   - For simplicity, create a small dataset directly in the script.

   - Alternatively, users can use a real dataset from a file.

2. Open Code Editor

   - Use preferred text editor or IDE.

3. Create a New Python File

   - Create a new file named "linear_regression.py."

Step 3: Implement the Linear Regression Model

1. Import Necessary Libraries

   - At the top of the *"linear_regression.py"* file, import the necessary libraries.

```
1    import pandas as pd
2    import numpy as np
3    from sklearn.model_selection import train_test_split
4    from sklearn.linear_model import LinearRegression
5    from sklearn.metrics import mean_squared_error, r2_score
6    import matplotlib.pyplot as plt
```

2. Create the Dataset

   - Define a small dataset within the script:

```
8    #Create the dataset
9    data = {
10   'Size': [1500, 1600, 1700, 1800, 1900, 2000, 2100, 2200, 2300, 2400],
11   'Price': [300000, 320000, 340000, 360000, 380000, 400000, 420000, 440000, 460000, 480000]
12   }
13   df = pd.DataFrame(data)
```

3. Preprocess the Data

- Split the data into input features (X) and target variable (Y).

- Split the data into training and testing sets.

```
15    # Preprocess the data
16    X = df[['Size']]
17    Y = df['Price']
18    X_train, X_test, Y_train, Y_test = train_test_split(X, Y, test_size=0.2, random_state=42)
```

4. Train the Model

- Create a linear regression model and train it on the training data:

```
20    # Train the model
21    model = LinearRegression()
22    model.fit(X_train, Y_train)
```

5. Evaluate the Model

- Make predictions on the test data.

- Calculate evaluation metrics:

```
24    # Evaluate the model
25    Y_pred = model.predict(X_test)
26    mse = mean_squared_error(Y_test, Y_pred)
27    r2 = r2_score(Y_test, Y_pred)
28    print(f"Mean Squared Error: {mse}")
29    print(f"R-squared: {r2}")
30
```

6. Visualize the Results

- Plot the training data, test data, and the regression line.

```
31    # Visualize the results
32    plt.scatter(X_train, Y_train, color='blue', label='Training data')
33    plt.scatter(X_test, Y_test, color='green', label='Test data')
34    plt.plot(X_test, Y_pred, color='red', linewidth=2, label='Regression line')
35    plt.xlabel('Size (sq ft)')
36    plt.ylabel('Price ($)')
37    plt.legend()
38    plt.show()
39
```

7. Complete Script

- The complete *"linear_regression.py"* file should look like this:

```
1    import pandas as pd
2    import numpy as np
3    from sklearn.model_selection import train_test_split
4    from sklearn.linear_model import LinearRegression
5    from sklearn.metrics import mean_squared_error, r2_score
6    import matplotlib.pyplot as plt
7
8    #Create the dataset
9    data = {
10   'Size': [1500, 1600, 1700, 1800, 1900, 2000, 2100, 2200, 2300, 2400],
11   'Price': [300000, 320000, 340000, 360000, 380000, 400000, 420000, 440000, 460000, 480000]
12   }
13   df = pd.DataFrame(data)
14
15   # Preprocess the data
16   X = df[['Size']]
17   Y = df['Price']
18   X_train, X_test, Y_train, Y_test = train_test_split(X, Y, test_size=0.2, random_state=42)
19
20   # Train the model
21   model = LinearRegression()
22   model.fit(X_train, Y_train)
23
24   # Evaluate the model
25   Y_pred = model.predict(X_test)
26   mse = mean_squared_error(Y_test, Y_pred)
27   r2 = r2_score(Y_test, Y_pred)
28   print(f"Mean Squared Error: {mse}")
29   print(f"R-squared: {r2}")
30
31   # Visualize the results
32   plt.scatter(X_train, Y_train, color='blue', label='Training data')
33   plt.scatter(X_test, Y_test, color='green', label='Test data')
34   plt.plot(X_test, Y_pred, color='red', linewidth=2, label='Regression line')
35   plt.xlabel('Size (sq ft)')
36   plt.ylabel('Price ($)')
37   plt.legend()
38   plt.show()
```

Step 4: Run the Script

1. Run the Script

   - Open a terminal or command prompt.

   - Navigate to the directory where the "linear_regression.py" file is located.

   - Run the script by typing:

     python3 linear_regression.py

2. View the Results

   - The script will print the mean squared error and R-squared values to the console.

- A plot will appear showing the training data, test data, and the regression line.

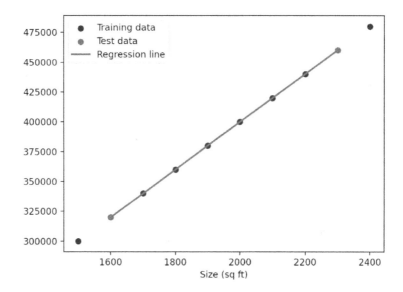

Following these steps results in a successfully implemented linear regression model to predict house prices. This exercise demonstrates the process of data preprocessing, model training, and evaluation, providing a practical understanding of how linear regression works in ML.

CONCLUSION

Understanding the foundational concepts and techniques of ML is indispensable for anyone aspiring to build effective AI systems. The sections in this chapter have methodically built upon each other, progressing from basic principles to more intricate applications and evaluations, laying a robust groundwork crucial for any AI practitioner. For those eager to explore deeper, further into specialized areas of ML such as deep learning and reinforcement learning is recommended. These advanced topics not only extend the foundational knowledge presented here but also open new possibilities for innovation and application in the field of AI. This chapter serves as both a beginning and an invitation to a broader journey into the ever-evolving world of AI.

## CHAPTER 3

DEEP LEARNING AND NEURAL NETWORKS

Deep learning, a subset of machine learning (ML) involving artificial neural networks (ANNs), is at the forefront of many recent breakthroughs in AI. This chapter examines the architecture and functioning of neural networks, including specialized forms like convolutional neural networks (CNNs) and recurrent neural networks (RNNs), as well as advanced models such as generative adversarial networks (GANs) and transformers. These neural network architectures have revolutionized the field of AI by enabling machines to process and interpret vast amounts of data with remarkable accuracy and efficiency.

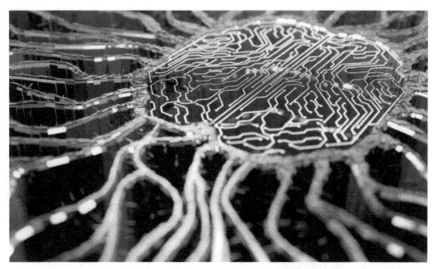

FIGURE 3.1 Conceptual representation of deep learning neural networks.

Figure 3.1 represents the concept of deep learning neural networks. The central structure, resembling a brain, is intricately connected by numerous pathways, symbolizing the complex neural network architectures used in deep learning. These pathways illustrate how data flows through multiple layers of interconnected neurons, mimicking the human brain's neural connections. The luminous circuits and connections highlight the vast and intricate processing capabilities of these networks, enabling them to learn and make decisions based on vast amounts of data. This depiction emphasizes the advanced, interconnected nature of deep learning models, which process information through multiple layers to identify patterns and generate insights, revolutionizing fields like image recognition, natural language processing (NLP), and autonomous systems.

Deep learning's transformative impact can be seen in its ability to perform complex tasks like image and speech recognition, where CNNs excel by efficiently processing grid-like data structures. RNNs, however, are adept at handling sequential data, making them ideal for applications in NLP and time-series prediction. Advanced models like GANs have opened new frontiers in data generation, creating realistic images, music, and even text by pitting two neural networks against each other in a creative adversarial process. Meanwhile, transformers have revolutionized the field of NLP by introducing mechanisms for attention, significantly improving the performance of language models and enabling groundbreaking applications such as language translation and text summarization. This chapter explores their applications and the computational principles that allow these networks to perform complex tasks, highlighting the continuous evolution and expanding capabilities of deep learning technologies.

INTRODUCTION TO DEEP LEARNING

Deep learning, an advanced branch of ML, utilizes deep neural networks to analyze large and complex data sets. This technique is essential for advancing AI, as it enables autonomous systems to perform sophisticated, multi-layered data interpretation. Deep learning models operate through multiple layers of artificial neurons, each layer designed to recognize different data aspects. As data progresses through these layers, the models become increasingly adept at making accurate predictions or classifications.

For example, in image recognition tasks, initial layers might focus on detecting simple edges and textures, while deeper layers identify complex shapes and objects. Similarly, in NLP, early layers might capture basic syntactic structures, whereas deeper layers understand semantic context and relationships. Despite its unparalleled accuracy in tasks such as image and speech recognition, deep learning requires significant computational power and extensive data sets, presenting challenges in terms of resource allocation and data privacy. Training these models often involves powerful graphical processing units (GPUs) or tensor processing units (TPUs) and large-scale data, which can be expensive and time-consuming to acquire. Additionally, the need for massive amounts of labeled data raises concerns about data privacy and security, as well as the potential for biases in the training data to affect the model's performance and fairness. As deep learning continues to evolve, addressing these challenges is crucial for its broader and more ethical application.

Understanding Neural Networks

Neural networks form the cornerstone of deep learning and are designed to simulate the way the human brain processes information.

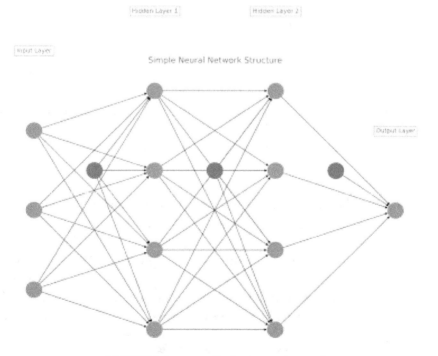

FIGURE 3.2 Structure of a simple neural network.

Figure 3.2 illustrates the structure of a simple neural network, high-lighting its key components and their interconnections. (*Note: The full color versions of all figures in this text, are available in the companion files.*) The green nodes on the left represent the input layer, where raw data enters the network, with each node corresponding to a feature in the dataset. The network includes multiple hidden layers of green nodes, where core processing occurs, receiving inputs from previous layers, processing them through weighted connections, and passing the results to subsequent layers. The blue node labeled "Bias" provides a constant input to neurons in both hidden and output layers, aiding in model fitting by adjusting outputs alongside weighted inputs. The green node on the right represents the output layer, which generates the final prediction or classification based on processed inputs. The black lines denote the connections between nodes in adjacent layers, each with an associated weight adjusted during training to minimize error and enhance model accuracy. This diagram underscores the flow of data from the input layer through hidden layers to the output layer, highlighting the roles of weights and biases in the learning and predic-tion processes.

Basic Structure

At the core of a neural network is the neuron, a unit that receives inputs, processes them using weights (which are adjustable parameters) and biases (constants added to the input), and passes the output through an activation function that determines whether and to what extent a signal should continue through the network. The structure of neural networks consists of multiple layers: an input layer, one or more hidden layers, and an output layer. Each layer is composed of neurons interconnected by weights, which adapt during training to minimize prediction errors.

How They Learn

Neural networks learn through a process known as backpropagation, where after output is produced, the network adjusts its weights and biases to minimize the error in prediction. This adjustment is facili-tated by optimization algorithms like gradient descent, which incre-mentally improves model parameters to reduce the loss function—a measure of how well the model's outputs match the expected outcomes. During training, the loss function's gradient is calculated, guiding the optimization process. By iteratively updating weights and biases in the direction that reduces the loss, the network learns to make accurate predictions.

Types of Neural Networks

Neural networks are characterized into the following:

Feedforward Neural Networks

The simplest type of ANN wherein connections between the nodes do not form a cycle. This type is used for basic classification and regression tasks. Each neuron in one layer is connected to every neuron in the subsequent layer, facilitating the flow of information strictly in one direction—from input to output.

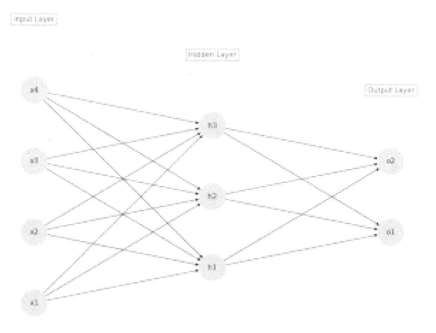

FIGURE 3.3 A feedforward neural network.

Figure 3.3 represents a feedforward neural network, highlighting its architecture and the flow of data through its layers. The network consists of three layers: the input layer, hidden layer, and output layer. The input layer contains four neurons (x1, x2, x3, x4), each representing a different feature of the input data. The hidden layer has three neurons (h1, h2, h3) that process the input features through weighted connections. Finally, the output layer includes two neurons (o1, o2) that generate the network's final predictions or classifications based on the processed information from the hidden layer. The arrows indicate the direction of data flow, showing how inputs are passed forward through the network, processed in the hidden layer, and result in outputs. This feedforward mechanism, where data moves in a single direction from input to output without looping back, is fundamental to many neural network models used in ML for tasks such as regression and classification.

Recurrent Neural Networks (RNNs)

Designed to manage sequential data, they can remember past information and use it to influence the current output, beneficial for tasks like language modeling and text generation. Recurrent neural networks (RNNs) have loops that allow information to persist, making them ideal for time series analysis and NLP tasks where the context of previous inputs is crucial for understanding the current input.

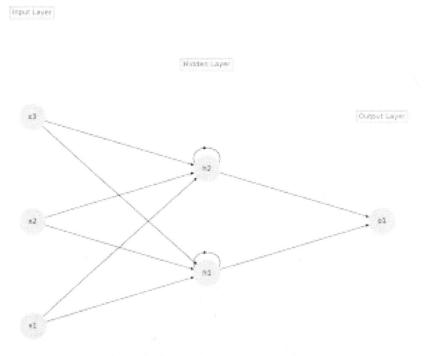

FIGURE 3.4 A recurrent neural network (RNN).

Figure 3.4 represents an RNN, illustrating the unique architecture that differentiates RNNs from feedforward networks. The network consists of input, hidden, and output layers. The key feature of RNNs is the presence of recurrent connections within the hidden layers, depicted by the looped arrows. These connections allow the network to maintain a memory of previous inputs by feeding the output of the hidden layer back into itself as input for the next time step. This mechanism enables the RNN to capture temporal dependencies and sequential patterns in data, making it well-suited for tasks such as time series analysis, NLP, and speech recognition. The diagram highlights how inputs are processed through the hidden layers, with recurrent connections enabling the network to leverage past information, producing an output that reflects both current and historical data.

Convolutional Neural Networks (CNNs)

Used in processing pixel data, these networks apply convolutional layers that filter inputs for useful information and are highly effective in areas such as image and video recognition tasks. Convolutional neural networks (CNNs) consist of convolutional layers, pooling layers, and fully connected layers. Convolutional layers apply filters to input data, detecting local patterns like edges in images. Pooling layers reduce the spatial dimensions of the data, enhancing computational efficiency and focusing on the most prominent features. Fully connected layers at the end of the network perform the final classification or regression based on the extracted features.

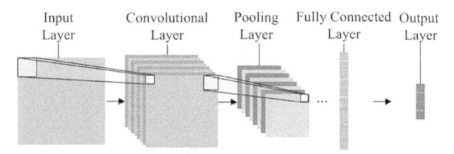

FIGURE 3.5 Architecture of a CNN.

Figure 3.5 illustrates the architecture of a CNN, highlighting the key layers and their roles in processing input data. The process begins with the input layer, where raw data, such as an image, is fed into the network. The data then passes through the convolutional layer, which applies convolutional filters to detect local patterns and features within the data, such as edges or textures. Following the convolution, the data enters the pooling layer, which reduces the spatial dimensions through operations like max pooling, thereby retaining prominent features while minimizing computational complexity. The processed data is then passed to the fully connected layer, where it is flattened and fed into a traditional neural network layer to perform high-level reasoning and make final predictions. Finally, the output layer produces the network's predictions, classifying the input data into specific categories. This layered structure, with convolution and pooling operations, makes CNNs particularly effective for tasks involving image and video analysis.

Additionally, there are more advanced types like *generative adversarial networks (GANs)*, which consist of two neural networks—the generator and the discriminator—that work against each other to create realistic synthetic data.

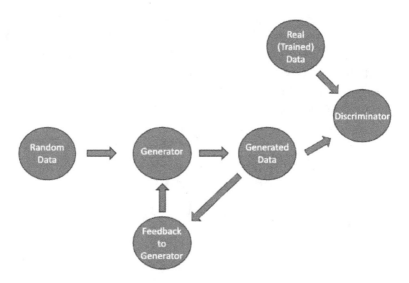

FIGURE 3.6 Architecture of GANs.

Figure 3.6 illustrates the architecture of GANs, a class of ML frameworks designed to generate realistic data. The process begins with random data, which is fed into the generator. The generator creates synthetic data samples that it tries to pass off as real. These generated samples are then evaluated by the discriminator, which also receives real data (trained data) for comparison. The discriminator's role is to distinguish between the real and generated data. It provides feedback to the generator, indicating how well it is performing in mimicking real data. This feedback loop allows the generator to improve its outputs iteratively. The three main steps are: (1) the generator creates data from random input, (2) the discriminator evaluates the generated data against real data, and (3) the discriminator provides feedback to the generator, which adjusts its parameters to produce more realistic data in future iterations. This adversarial process continues until the generator produces highly realistic data that the discriminator cannot easily differentiate from the real data.

Transformers

Transformers, another advanced architecture, utilize self-attention mechanisms to process sequential data more efficiently than RNNs, excelling in tasks like language translation and summarization. Understanding these diverse types of neural networks and their specific applications is key to leveraging their full potential in solving complex problems.

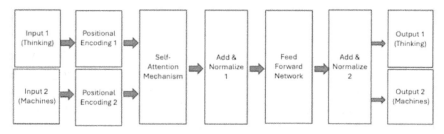

FIGURE 3.7 Architecture of a transformer model.

Figure 3.7 illustrates the architecture of a transformer model, specifically highlighting the encoder component used in NLP tasks. It demonstrates the process of encoding two words, "Thinking" and "Machines," by converting them into numerical representations that include positional encoding to capture the sequence order. Within the encoder, multiple layers perform key functions: the self-attention mechanism weighs the importance of different words relative to each other, enabling the model to focus on relevant words; add and normalize operations stabilize and speed up training by normalizing the outputs and inputs; and feed forward networks capture complex relationships by further processing the data. The figure highlights how data flows through these layers, showing the intricate process by which the transformer model encodes information to generate meaningful representations of the input words.

Key Architectures in Deep Learning

This sublesson focuses on advanced neural network architectures that have been pivotal in the field of deep learning:

CNNs

CNNs are specialized deep neural networks designed to process data with a grid-like topology, such as images. A distinguishing feature of CNNs is their use of convolutional layers, which apply convolutional filters to the input data. These filters capture spatial hierarchies of features, starting with simple patterns like edges in the lower layers and progressing to more complex shapes and objects in the higher layers. This hierarchical feature extraction allows CNNs to effectively recognize and classify images, making them indispensable in computer vision tasks such as image recognition, object detection, and image segmentation.

RNNs

RNNs are designed to manage sequential data and have a unique memory feature that stores information from previous inputs. This memory capability makes RNNs ideal for applications where the sequence and context of the data are crucial, such as speech recognition, language modeling, and music generation. However, standard RNNs face challenges like vanishing and exploding gradients, which hinder their performance on long sequences. To address these issues, variants like long short-term memory LSTM and gated recurrent units (GRU) have been developed. These variants include mechanisms to maintain long-term dependencies and manage gradient flow more effectively.

Transformers

Transformers, introduced in the seminal paper *"Attention Is All You Need,"* (Authors: Ashish Vaswani, Noam Shazeer, Niki Parmar, Jakob Uszkoreit, Llion Jones, Aidan N. Gomez, Łukasz Kaiser, Illia Polosukhin) have revolutionized NLP by becoming the foundation for many state-of-the-art models. Unlike RNNs, which process data sequentially, transformers use self-attention mechanisms to weigh the importance of different words in a sentence, regardless of their positions. This allows transformers to capture long-range dependencies and contextual relationships more effectively. The ability to process entire sequences in parallel also makes transformers more computationally efficient. Consequently, they have been instrumental in advancing tasks such as machine translation, text summarization, and sentiment analysis, leading to models like BERT and GPT.

Challenges and Ethical Considerations

Deep learning is not without its challenges and ethical implications, which need careful consideration.

Computational Demands

Deep learning models, particularly those with many layers, require significant computational power to train efficiently. This often necessitates the use of specialized hardware like GPUs or TPUs. These units are designed to manage the massive parallel processing tasks that deep learning models demand. Computational demands also extend to memory requirements and data throughput, necessitating high-performance computing environments. Efficient training of large models can lead to substantial energy consumption, prompting ongoing research into optimizing algorithms and hardware to reduce the environmental impact and improve energy efficiency.

Data Requirements

The effectiveness of deep learning models is heavily dependent on the quantity and quality of the training data. Large, diverse datasets enable models to generalize better and perform accurately across various tasks. However, data issues such as biases, inaccuracies, or insufficient diversity can lead to flawed model predictions and ethical concerns. To address data scarcity and enhance diversity, strategies like data augmentation, which involves creating new training examples by modifying existing ones, and synthetic data generation, where artificial data is generated to simulate real-world conditions, are commonly employed. Ensuring high-quality, representative datasets is crucial for the development of robust deep learning models.

Privacy and Security

With the increasing use of deep learning across various sectors, concerns about privacy and security are paramount. Sensitive data, such as personal information and proprietary business data, must be protected from unauthorized access and misuse. Techniques like federated learning, where training occurs across multiple decentralized devices without exchanging raw data samples, help maintain data privacy by keeping data local. Differential privacy, another critical approach, adds controlled noise to datasets to obscure individual identities while still enabling meaningful analysis. These techniques are essential in mitigating privacy risks and ensuring that deep learning applications comply with regulatory standards and ethical guidelines.

ARTIFICIAL NEURAL NETWORKS (ANNS)

Artificial neural networks (ANNs) are composed of interconnected groups of nodes or neurons, simplifying, and mimicking the human brain's structure. These networks are organized into layers that process inputs and generate outputs based on computational functions. ANNs are trained using algorithms such as backpropagation, where the system adjusts its weights after each output to minimize error rates in predictions, all guided by a selected loss function. In practical applications, ANNs are employed across various sectors, enhancing efficiency and accuracy in tasks like credit scoring in the finance industry, providing diagnostic assistance in healthcare, improving supply chain optimization in logistics, and even enabling personalized recommendations in e-commerce platforms. Their versatility and robustness make them a cornerstone technology in the advancement of AI-driven solutions.

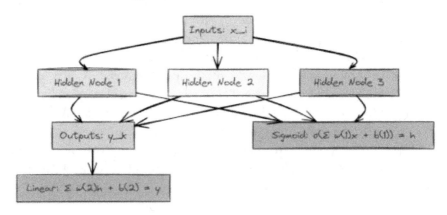

FIGURE 3.8 An artificial neural network (ANN) architecture.

Figure 3.8 illustrates an ANN architecture, which consists of an input layer, a hidden layer, and an output layer. The input layer receives inputs that are fed into the network. These inputs are processed through the hidden layer, where each neuron computes a weighted sum of its inputs and applies a sigmoid activation function ($\sigma\sigma$), transforming the input data into an intermediate representation. The connections between neurons in adjacent layers are represented by weights. The output layer takes the outputs from the hidden layer and applies a linear activation function to produce the final outputs. The equations at the bottom illustrate the mathematical operations performed within the hidden and output layers, showing how the inputs are transformed through weighted sums and activation functions to produce the network's outputs. This ANN model exemplifies the process by which neural networks learn to map inputs to outputs, enabling tasks such as classification and prediction.

Fundamentals of ANNs

Neuron Model

Each neuron in an ANN receives input from data or other neurons, processes it using a weighted sum, and then passes this sum through an activation function. The activation function determines the neuron's output by introducing nonlinearity, allowing the network to learn and model complex patterns. This output is then transmitted to subsequent neurons, enabling the network to build hierarchical representations of the input data. Neurons are the fundamental units of an ANN, and their collective interactions determine the network's capability to perform tasks such as classification, regression, and more.

Layers of an ANN

ANNs are structured into three types of layers: input, hidden, and output. The input layer receives raw data and passes it onto the hidden layers. The hidden layers, often comprising multiple layers, perform most of the computational work by processing and transforming the input data through interconnected neurons. These layers extract and learn intricate features from the data. The output layer produces the results of the ANN, such as classification labels or predicted values. This layered structure allows ANNs to model and solve complex problems by learning hierarchical features of the input data.

Activation Functions

Common activation functions in ANNs include sigmoid, tanh, and ReLU (rectified linear unit). The sigmoid function maps input values to a range between 0 and 1, making it useful for binary classification tasks. The tanh function maps inputs to a range between -1 and 1, providing stronger gradients for learning. The ReLU function, which outputs the input directly if it is positive and zero otherwise, helps in mitigating the vanishing gradient problem, allowing networks to learn faster and perform better. These functions play crucial roles in helping neural networks learn and represent complex patterns during training, contributing to the network's overall performance and accuracy.

Training Neural Networks

Training neural networks is done through the following functions:

Backpropagation

Backpropagation is a fundamental method for training ANNs. It adjusts the weights of connections in the network by propagating errors backward from the output layer toward the input layer. This process involves computing the gradient of the loss function with respect to each weight by applying the chain rule of calculus. By iteratively updating the weights in the direction that reduces the error, backpropagation enables the network to learn and improve its performance on the given task. This method is crucial for effectively training deep neural networks and achieving high accuracy in various applications.

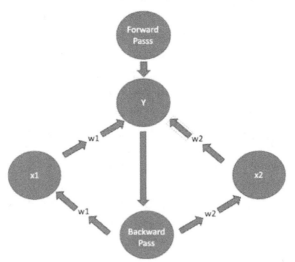

FIGURE 3.9 A simple neural network to explain backpropagation.

Figure 3.9 illustrates a simple neural network used to explain the concept of backpropagation. The network consists of an input layer with two input neurons (x1 and $x2$) and an output layer with one output neuron (y). Each input neuron is connected to the output neuron through weights ($w1$ and $w2$). In backpropagation, the network initially performs a forward pass where the inputs are multiplied by their respective weights and summed to produce the output. The error is then calculated by comparing the network's output with the true value. During the backward pass, the error is propagated back through the network, and the weights are adjusted to minimize this error. This iterative process of forward and backward passes allows the network to learn from the data by gradually optimizing the weights to improve prediction accuracy.

Loss Functions

Loss functions are critical in evaluating how well an ANN's output matches the expected results. Distinct types of loss functions are used depending on the nature of the task. Mean squared error (MSE) is commonly used for regression tasks, measuring the average squared difference between predicted and actual values. Cross-entropy loss, often used for classification tasks, quantifies the difference between the predicted probability distribution and the actual distribution. These loss functions guide the training process by providing a measure of the model's performance, which is then minimized through optimization algorithms to improve accuracy.

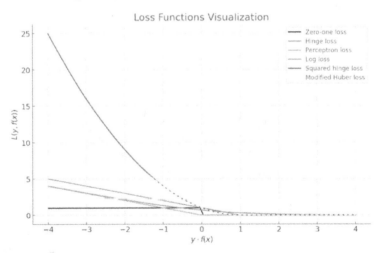

FIGURE 3.10 Various loss functions used in ML.

Figure 3.10 illustrates various loss functions used in ML to quantify the difference between the predicted values and the actual values. (*Note: The full color versions of all figures in this text, are available in the companion files.*) The loss functions depicted include zero-one loss, hinge loss, perceptron loss, log loss, squared hinge loss, and modified

Huber loss. Each loss function has a unique curve representing how the loss value changes with respect to the difference between the true value yy and the predicted value)$f(x)$. The zero-one loss (black) represents a simple misclassification error, hinge loss (green) is commonly used in support vector machines, perceptron loss (purple) is used in perceptron algorithms, log loss (red) is used in logistic regression, squared hinge loss (blue) is a variation of hinge loss, and modified Huber loss (yellow) is a smooth approximation to the hinge loss. Understanding these loss functions is crucial for selecting the appropriate model and training algorithms to minimize prediction errors.

Optimization Algorithms

Optimization algorithms are essential for minimizing the loss function and efficiently updating the weights during training. Stochastic gradient descent (SGD) is a basic but powerful algorithm that updates weights incrementally using a subset of the training data. Adaptive moment estimation (ADAM) combines the advantages of two other extensions of SGD, providing an adaptive learning rate for each parameter by estimating the first and second moments of the gradients. RMSprop (root mean square propagation) adjusts the learning rate for each weight based on the recent magnitude of gradients, helping to maintain steady progress during training. These algorithms are crucial for effectively training neural networks, ensuring convergence to optimal solutions.

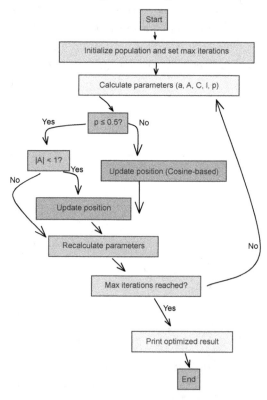

FIGURE 3.11 An optimization algorithm demonstrating the workflow of a whale optimization algorithm (WOA).

Figure 3.11 illustrates an optimization algorithm, specifically demonstrating the workflow of a whale optimization algorithm (WOA). The process begins with initializing the population and setting the maximum number of iterations. The algorithm iterates through a loop where it calculates certain parameters (a, A, C, l, and p) for the whale population. Depending on the value of p, the algorithm decides between different update strategies. If $p \leq 0.5p \leq 0.5$, it further checks if the absolute value of A is less than 1 to determine the next position of the whales. If $p > 0.5p > 0.5$, it uses a cosine-based position update method. This iterative process continues, adjusting whale positions and recalculating parameters, until the maximum number of iterations is reached. The final optimized result is printed at the end. This figure exemplifies the use of heuristic and bio-inspired optimization techniques in solving complex optimization problems.

Practical Applications of ANNs

The following sections describe some practical applications of ANNs.

Finance

ANNs play a pivotal role in finance by leveraging their ability to analyze vast amounts of data and detect intricate patterns. They are extensively used to predict stock market trends by analyzing historical price movements, market sentiment, and other financial indicators. In credit scoring, ANNs assess the creditworthiness of individuals by evaluating various financial parameters and behavioral patterns, offering more accurate predictions than traditional methods. Additionally, ANNs are instrumental in fraud detection, where they analyze transaction data in real-time to identify anomalies that may indicate fraudulent activities, thus enhancing the security of financial systems.

Healthcare

In the healthcare sector, ANNs significantly improve diagnostic accuracy and patient outcomes by analyzing medical images and other health data. For instance, in medical imaging, ANNs are used to identify patterns that indicate the presence of diseases such as cancer in mammography or diabetic retinopathy in retinal scans. These networks can detect subtle features in the images that might be missed by human eyes, enabling early diagnosis and better treatment planning. Furthermore, ANNs are used to predict patient outcomes, personalize treatment plans, and streamline administrative tasks, thereby improving the overall efficiency and effectiveness of healthcare delivery.

Industrial Automation

ANNs are revolutionizing industrial automation by optimizing production processes and enhancing quality control. In predictive maintenance, ANNs analyze data from sensors and machinery to predict when equipment is likely to fail, allowing for timely maintenance and reducing downtime. This predictive capability helps in minimizing operational disruptions and extending the lifespan of machinery. In quality control, ANNs detect manufacturing defects by analyzing data from various stages of the production process. By identifying faults early, these networks help maintain lofty standards of product quality and reduce waste, leading to more efficient and cost-effective manufacturing operations.

CNNS

CNNs are tailored for processing visual data, using convolutional layers to effectively filter and prioritize information from pixel data. These networks implement a hierarchical layer structure that processes inputs through various transformations and pooling, reducing dimensionality while preserving essential features required for accurate image classification. In industry, CNNs play a crucial role, underpinning technologies such as facial recognition systems in security and enhancing diagnostic imagery in the medical field, thereby significantly advancing the capabilities of both sectors.

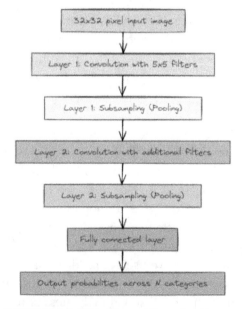

FIGURE 3.12 A CNN with a multilayered architecture.

Figure 3.12 exemplifies a CNN with a multilayered architecture for image processing and classification. Starting with a 32x32 pixel input image, the network includes Layer 1, which performs convolution operations using 5x5 filters to generate feature maps, followed by subsampling (or pooling) layers to reduce spatial dimensions while preserving noteworthy features. Layer 2 continues this process with additional convolution and subsampling layers, abstracting the input features into higher level representations. The final classifier section involves a fully connected layer that integrates these features and outputs probabilities across N categories, representing the final image classification. This structured approach enables CNNs to effectively recognize complex patterns and deliver accurate image classifications.

Architecture of CNNs

The following sections describe what Architectures of CNNs are comprised of.

Convolutional Layers

Convolutional layers are a fundamental component of CNNs. These layers employ filters or kernels that slide over the input image to perform convolution operations, extracting essential features such as edges, colors, and textures. Each filter is designed to detect unique features at various spatial hierarchies, starting from low-level features like edges and progressing to more complex patterns like shapes and objects. By capturing these hierarchical features, convolutional layers enhance the network's ability to recognize and distinguish complex patterns within the data, contributing to high accuracy in tasks such as image and video recognition.

Pooling Layers

Pooling layers, which typically follow convolutional layers, play a crucial role in reducing the spatial size of the representation. This reduction decreases the number of parameters and the amount of computation required in the network, thereby improving efficiency. Pooling, often implemented as max pooling, helps make the detection of features invariant to scale and orientation changes. For example, max pooling takes the maximum value from each region covered by the filter, ensuring that the most prominent features are retained while reducing the dimensionality of the data. This process helps in preserving key features while discarding less relevant information, enhancing the network's robustness and generalization capabilities.

Fully Connected Layers

Fully connected layers serve as classifiers on top of the extracted features from the convolutional and pooling layers. These layers take the flattened outputs from the previous layers and learn nonlinear combinations of these features to determine the class of the input image. By connecting every neuron in one layer to every neuron in the next, fully connected layers can integrate and interpret the high-level features extracted by the convolutional layers. This integration enables the network to make final predictions, such as classifying an image into distinct categories. Fully connected layers are essential for translating the learned features into meaningful outputs, completing the neural network's process of recognition and classification.

Functionality and Training of CNNs

The following sections describe functionality and training of CNNs.

Feature Learning

Feature learning in CNNs is a major advantage over traditional algorithms that require manual feature design. Unlike these traditional methods, CNNs automatically learn increasingly complex features directly from the data. The initial layers of a CNN focus on capturing basic features such as edges and simple textures. As the data progresses through the network, the subsequent deeper layers identify more complex features, such as shapes, patterns, and eventually specific objects or parts of objects. This hierarchical feature extraction allows CNNs to effectively learn and generalize from raw data, improving their performance in tasks like image classification, object detection, and facial recognition.

Backpropagation in CNNs

Backpropagation in CNNs is a critical process for training the network. During this process, CNNs adjust the filters' weights to optimize their performance. This adjustment is achieved by propagating the error, calculated as the difference between the actual and predicted outputs, back through the network. The backpropagation algorithm computes the gradient of the loss function with respect to each weight, enabling the optimization algorithm, such as gradient descent, to update the weights in a way that minimizes the loss function. This iterative process continues until the network achieves the desired level of accuracy, allowing the CNN to learn and improve its predictions over time.

Advanced Training Techniques

Advanced training techniques are employed to enhance the performance and efficiency of CNNs. One such technique is dropout, which involves randomly dropping a proportion of neurons during training. This prevents the network from becoming too reliant on specific neurons, thereby reducing overfitting and improving generalization to new data. Another crucial technique is batch normalization, which normalizes the inputs of each layer by adjusting and scaling the activations. This not only accelerates the training process but also stabilizes the learning by reducing internal covariate shift. These advanced techniques, among others, are essential for optimizing the training dynamics and overall performance of CNNs, making them more robust and effective in various applications.

Real-World Applications of CNNs

The following sections describe some real-world applications of CNNs.

Facial Recognition Systems

CNNs are fundamental in developing systems that require facial recognition capabilities. These networks are extensively used in security systems to enhance surveillance by accurately identifying and verifying individuals in real-time. Facial recognition systems powered by CNNs are also integrated into smartphones and other personal devices for user authentication, providing a secure and convenient method for unlocking devices and accessing sensitive information. By learning and recognizing intricate facial features, CNNs ensure high accuracy and reliability in diverse lighting conditions and varying angles, making them indispensable in modern security and authentication solutions.

Medical Imaging

In the medical field, CNNs are crucial for analyzing several types of imaging data. They are used to detect tumors in MRI scans by identifying abnormal patterns that indicate the presence of cancer. Additionally, CNNs aid in the diagnosis of a wide range of diseases through pattern recognition in pathological images, such as identifying signs of diabetic retinopathy in retinal images or classifying distinct types of lung infections in chest X-rays. By automating the analysis of medical images, CNNs significantly enhance diagnostic accuracy, reduce the workload on medical professionals, and facilitate early detection and treatment of diseases.

Automotive Industry

CNNs play a vital role in the development of autonomous driving technologies. In this industry, CNNs are used to interpret continuous video data from cameras mounted on vehicles, enabling them to recognize and classify objects such as pedestrians, traffic signs, and other vehicles. This real-time analysis allows autonomous vehicles to make informed decisions about navigation, lane changes, and obstacle avoidance. By processing and understanding the visual environment, CNNs help ensure the safety and efficiency of self-driving cars, contributing to advancements in intelligent transportation systems and the future of autonomous mobility.

RNNS

RNNs are uniquely designed to process sequential data, capturing information in their hidden layers from previous inputs to influence future processing. To tackle usual challenges like the vanishing gradient problem, RNNs utilize complex structures such as LSTM units and GRUs, which help maintain learning stability over long sequences. These networks are extensively used across various applications, including language translation services, voice-activated assistants, and financial forecasting, demonstrating their versatility and critical role in sequential data analysis.

Handling Sequential Data

RNNs are distinct in their ability to connect previous information to the current task, which is crucial for processing sequences of data such as spoken language, written text, or time series data. This sequential processing capability allows RNNs to maintain contextual information over time, making them ideally suited for applications where context is important. For instance, in NLP, RNNs can understand the entire sentence by remembering previous words, which is essential for accurate language translation or sentiment analysis. In financial analysis, RNNs can predict the next stock movement by analyzing historical stock prices and identifying trends over time, thereby providing valuable insights for trading strategies. This ability to handle sequential dependencies and temporal patterns makes RNNs versatile tools in various domains requiring context-aware analysis and prediction.

Advanced Architectures

To address challenges like the vanishing gradient problem, which can occur in standard RNNs due to the exponential shrinking of gradients during backpropagation through time, RNNs often incorporate advanced structures like LSTM units or GRUs.

LSTMs are designed to preserve the error signal that can be back-propagated through time and layers by maintaining a more constant error flow. They achieve this through a sophisticated gating mechanism consisting of input, output, and forget gates that regulate the flow of information and manage the cell state, enabling the network to retain or discard information as needed. This helps in learning long-term dependencies, making LSTMs highly effective for tasks such as speech recognition, language translation, and time series forecasting.

GRUs, however, simplify the LSTM design by combining several gates into one, reducing the complexity of the model without a significant loss of capability. GRUs use two gates—a reset gate and an update gate—to control the flow of information. The reset gate determines how much of the past information to forget, while the update gate decides how much of the latest information to pass to the output. This streamlined structure allows GRUs to perform comparably to LSTMs in many tasks, with the added benefit of faster training and reduced computational overhead. Both LSTMs and GRUs have become essential components in addressing the limitations of traditional RNNs, facilitating more robust and efficient learning in sequential data processing.

Applications of RNNs

The following sections describe some applications of RNNs.

Language Translation Services

RNNs are used extensively in machine translation, particularly in sequence-to-sequence models. These models excel at capturing sentence structures and context, enabling them to translate text from one language to another with high accuracy. RNNs can manage the nuances of different languages, ensuring that translations are not just word-for-word but contextually appropriate, making them essential in applications like Google Translate and other language services.

Voice-Activated Assistants

RNNs are integral to developing voice recognition systems that underpin popular voice-activated assistants like Siri, Alexa, and Google Assistant. They process the audio signal over time, picking up nuances of speech that evolve over several periods. By understanding the temporal dynamics of spoken language, RNNs enable these assistants to accurately recognize and respond to voice commands, enhancing user interaction and accessibility.

Financial Forecasting

In finance, RNNs analyze sequential data for tasks such as stock price predictions, risk assessment, and other time-series forecasting activities. RNNs are adept at understanding patterns over time, making them invaluable for financial analysis that requires a temporal prediction model. Their ability to process and interpret sequential data helps in predicting market trends, assessing financial risks, and making informed investment decisions.

RNNs have proven to be indispensable in fields that require the analysis of sequential data, highlighting their flexibility and effectiveness in handling tasks that involve complex temporal dependencies.

ADVANCED ARCHITECTURES (FOR EXAMPLE, GANS, TRANSFORMERS)

GANs feature a dual-model framework, comprising a generator and a discriminator, which compete against each other to produce synthetic data instances that closely mimic real data. Alternatively, transformers dramatically enhance the speed and efficiency of sequence processing through an attention mechanism, making them particularly effective for managing large language models. Together, GANs and transformers have significantly expanded AI's capabilities, facilitated the creation of realistic synthetic media and improved machines' understanding of human language, respectively.

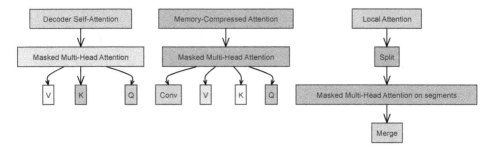

FIGURE 3.13 Advanced neural network architectures.

Figure 3.13 illustrates advanced neural network architectures with a focus on distinct types of attention mechanisms used in models such as transformers. The first section, decoder self-attention, highlights masked multi head attention where the attention mechanism processes input sequences by attending to various positions within the same sequence, which is crucial for sequence-to-sequence tasks like translation. The second section, memory-compressed attention, demonstrates a variant where the attention mechanism uses convolutional operations to compress memory, enhancing efficiency by reducing the computational load. The third section, local attention, splits the input into smaller segments, applies masked multihead attention to each segment, and then merges the results, optimizing the model's ability to focus on local patterns. These sophisticated attention mechanisms are integral to the functionality of advanced architectures like transformers, enabling them to handle complex tasks involving long-range dependencies and dynamic data interactions.

GANs

GANs revolutionize the generation of new, synthetic data by employing two neural networks in a competitive framework.

Figure 3.14 represents a GAN architecture, highlighting the discriminator model. The process starts with an input image of size 32x32x3 (representing width, height, and color channels). The image is passed through three convolutional layers (conv1, conv2, conv3), each followed by batch normalization and Leaky ReLU activation functions to enhance learning and stability. The first convolutional layer (conv1) has 128 filters, the second (conv2) has 256 filters, and the third (conv3) has 512 filters. These layers progressively reduce the spatial dimensions while increasing the depth, extracting high-level features from the input image. After flattening the output from the final convolutional layer, it is passed to a fully connected layer, and a sigmoid activation function is applied to produce a binary output indicating whether the input image is real (1) or fake (0). This setup is essential in the GAN framework, where the discriminator learns to distinguish between real images from the training dataset and fake images generated by the generator, improving the generator's ability to produce realistic images.

Generator

The *generator* in a GAN is a neural network designed to learn to generate plausible data that mimics the real dataset. Initially, the generator produces random data, but over time, through continuous training, it learns to create data instances that are increasingly difficult

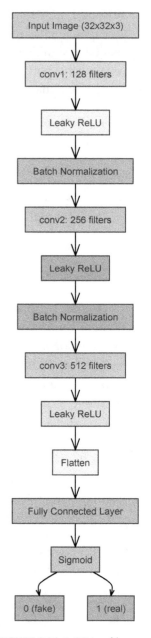

FIGURE 3.14 A GAN architecture.

to distinguish from actual data. The generator's training process involves learning to fool the discriminator, another neural network in the GAN, into believing that the generated data is real. As the generator improves, it refines its ability to create highly realistic data, such as images, text, or other forms of synthetic data.

Discriminator

The discriminator in a GAN is a neural network tasked with distinguishing between real data from the training set and synthetic data produced by the generator. Acting like a critic, the discriminator evaluates each data instance and assigns a probability score indicating whether it is real or fake. By providing feedback to the generator, the discriminator pushes the generator to produce more convincing outputs. The discriminator's role is crucial as it continuously challenges the generator, ensuring that the synthetic data becomes progressively more realistic through this adversarial process.

Training Process

The training process of GANs involves an alternating optimization approach where the generator and discriminator networks are trained in a competitive manner. First, the discriminator is trained to accurately differentiate between real and fake data, optimizing its ability to detect synthetic data produced by the generator. Next, the generator is trained to produce data that can fool the discriminator, optimizing its parameters to generate more realistic outputs. This back-and-forth adjustment, known as adversarial training, continues until the generator produces data that is indistinguishable from real data, significantly enhancing the quality of the generated outputs.

Applications

GANs have a wide range of applications across various fields. They are used to create highly realistic photographs and enhance image resolution, making them valuable in fields like photography and video production. GANs also simulate 3D models of environments for virtual reality and gaming, providing immersive experiences. In the art world, GANs generate novel artworks by learning from existing styles and techniques. Additionally, in drug discovery, GANs help model molecular structures, facilitating the design of new pharmaceuticals by predicting how different compounds might interact. These diverse applications highlight the transformative potential of GANs in generating innovative and useful data across multiple domains.

Transformers

Transformers are a type of deep learning model that has set new standards in the ability to handle sequences of data, particularly for tasks involving NLP.

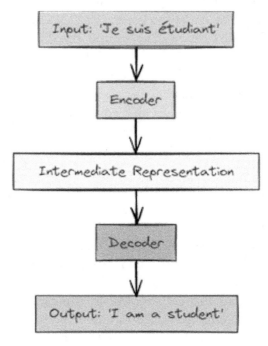

FIGURE 3.15 Architecture of a transformer model.

Figure 3.15 illustrates the architecture of a transformer model, specifically in the context of machine translation. The process begins with the input sentence "Je suis étudiant" in French. This input is fed into the encoder component, which processes and transforms the input data into an intermediate representation. The encoders consist of multiple layers that apply self-attention mechanisms and feed-forward neural networks to capture the context and relationships within the input sentence. This intermediate representation is then passed to the decoder component, which translates the encoded information into the target language, producing the output sentence "I am a student" in English. The decoders also utilize self-attention and feed-forward layers, along with mechanisms to address the encoder's outputs, ensuring the translation is contextually accurate. This figure exemplifies how transformers efficiently manage language translation tasks by leveraging the powerful attention mechanisms in both the encoder and decoder components.

Core Mechanism

Unlike traditional sequence processing models like RNNs or LSTMs, transformers use an attention mechanism that processes an entire sequence simultaneously. This mechanism allows the model to weigh the importance of different words within a sentence, regardless of their positional distance from each other. By focusing on relevant parts of the input sequence, the attention mechanism enables transformers to capture long-range dependencies and contextual relationships more effectively, leading to better performance in tasks involving complex data structures and long sequences.

Training Efficiency

By leveraging attention mechanisms and parallel processing capabilities, transformers can be trained more efficiently on large datasets. This parallelism allows for the simultaneous processing of sequence elements, significantly speeding up the training process. Transformers can quickly adapt to new or unseen data, making them highly effective for tasks in dynamic environments. Their ability to manage large volumes of data and learn intricate patterns rapidly contributes to their superiority in performance and scalability compared to traditional models.

Applications

Transformers are foundational for models like Google's BERT (bidirectional encoder representations from transformers) and OpenAI's GPT (generative pretrained transformer) series. These models have significantly advanced the state of the art in NLP tasks such as machine translation, text summarization, and sentiment analysis. Their robust architecture enables them to understand and generate human-like text, improving applications like chatbots, search engines, and recommendation systems. The versatility and power of transformer models continue to drive innovation and breakthroughs in NLP and other AI fields.

Both GANs and transformers have dramatically expanded the frontiers of what is possible with AI, each in their unique way. GANs push the boundaries in generating new, realistic synthetic data, helping in fields like media creation and scientific research. Meanwhile, transformers have revolutionized how machines understand and generate human language, providing tools that can interpret and respond to textual data with a high degree of fluency and context awareness. Together, these advanced architectures continue to facilitate significant innovations in AI, driving both practical applications and academic research forward.

AI APPLICATION: BUILD A BASIC NEURAL NETWORK FOR DIGIT CLASSIFICATION USING MNIST DATASET

In this AI application, users will build a basic neural network for digit classification using the MNIST dataset. This guide provides step-by-step instructions for creating, training, and evaluating a neural network using Python and TensorFlow/Keras, including:

- *Step 1*: Set Up the Development Environment
- *Step 2*: Load and Preprocess the MNIST Dataset
- *Step 3*: Create the Neural Network
- *Step 4*: Train the Neural Network
- *Step 5*: Evaluate the Model
- *Step 6*: Run the Script

Step 1: Set Up the Development Environment

1. Install Python

    a. Follow the instructions in the previous examples to download and install Python.

2. Install Necessary Libraries

    a. Open a terminal or command prompt.
    b. Install TensorFlow and Keras by typing:
    pip install tensorflow

Step 2: Load and Preprocess the MNIST Dataset

1. Open the Code Editor

    a. Use preferred text editor or IDE.

2. Create a New Python File

    a. Create a new file named *"mnist_nn.py."*

3. Import Necessary Libraries

   a. At the top of the *"mnist_nn.py"* file, import the necessary libraries:

```
1   import tensorflow as tf
2   from tensorflow.keras.models import Sequential
3   from tensorflow.keras.layers import Dense, Flatten
4   from tensorflow.keras.utils import to_categorical
5   import matplotlib.pyplot as plt
6   import numpy as np
```

4. Load the MNIST Dataset

   a. Load the dataset and split it into training and testing sets:

```
8    # Load the MNIST dataset from a local file
9    path = '/Users/erikherman/Documents/GitHub/PublicInformationLimited/AI_Revealed/mnist.npz'
10   with np.load(path) as data:
11       X_train = data['x_train']
12       Y_train = data['y_train']
13       X_test = data['x_test']
14       Y_test = data['y_test']
```

5. Preprocess the Data

   a. Normalize the input data by scaling pixel values to the range [0, 1].
   b. Convert the labels to one-hot encoded vectors.

```
16   # Preprocess the data
17   X_train = X_train.astype('float32') / 255
18   X_test = X_test.astype('float32') / 255
19   Y_train = to_categorical(Y_train, 10)
20   Y_test = to_categorical(Y_test, 10)
```

Step 3: Create the Neural Network

1. Build the Model

   a. Create a sequential model and add layers.

```
22   # Build the model
23   model = Sequential([
24       Flatten(input_shape=(28, 28)),
25       Dense(128, activation='relu'),
26       Dense(10, activation='softmax')
27   ])
```

2. Compile the Model

    a. Compile the model with an appropriate optimizer, loss function, and metrics.

```
29    # Compile the model
30    model.compile(optimizer='adam', loss='categorical_crossentropy', metrics=['accuracy'])
```

Step 4: Train the Neural Network

1. Train the Model

    a. Train the model on the training data.

```
32    # Train the model
33    history = model.fit(X_train, Y_train, epochs=10, validation_split=0.2)
```

Step 5: Evaluate the Model

1. Evaluate the Model

    a. Evaluate the model on the test data.

```
35    # Evaluate the model
36    test_loss, test_accuracy = model.evaluate(X_test, Y_test)
37    print(f"Test accuracy: {test_accuracy}")
```

2. Visualize Training History

    a. Plot the training and validation accuracy over epochs.

```
39    # Visualize training history
40    plt.plot(history.history['accuracy'], label='Training accuracy')
41    plt.plot(history.history['val_accuracy'], label='Validation accuracy')
42    plt.xlabel('Epoch')
43    plt.ylabel('Accuracy')
44    plt.legend()
45    plt.show()
```

1. Complete Script

a. The complete "mnist_nn.py" file should look like this.

```
1   import tensorflow as tf
2   from tensorflow.keras.models import Sequential
3   from tensorflow.keras.layers import Dense, Flatten
4   from tensorflow.keras.utils import to_categorical
5   import matplotlib.pyplot as plt
6   import numpy as np
7
8   # Load the MNIST dataset from a local file
9   path = '/Users/erikherman/Documents/GitHub/PublicInformationLimited/AI_Revealed/mnist.npz'
10  with np.load(path) as data:
11      X_train = data['x_train']
12      Y_train = data['y_train']
13      X_test = data['x_test']
14      Y_test = data['y_test']
15
16  # Preprocess the data
17  X_train = X_train.astype('float32') / 255
18  X_test = X_test.astype('float32') / 255
19  Y_train = to_categorical(Y_train, 10)
20  Y_test = to_categorical(Y_test, 10)
21
22  # Build the model
23  model = Sequential([
24      Flatten(input_shape=(28, 28)),
25      Dense(128, activation='relu'),
26      Dense(10, activation='softmax')
27  ])
28
29  # Compile the model
30  model.compile(optimizer='adam', loss='categorical_crossentropy', metrics=['accuracy'])
31
32  # Train the model
33  history = model.fit(X_train, Y_train, epochs=10, validation_split=0.2)
34
35  # Evaluate the model
36  test_loss, test_accuracy = model.evaluate(X_test, Y_test)
37  print(f"Test accuracy: {test_accuracy}")
38
39  # Visualize training history
40  plt.plot(history.history['accuracy'], label='Training accuracy')
41  plt.plot(history.history['val_accuracy'], label='Validation accuracy')
42  plt.xlabel('Epoch')
43  plt.ylabel('Accuracy')
44  plt.legend()
45  plt.show()
```

Step 6: Run the Script

1. Run the Script

a. Open a terminal or command prompt.

b. Navigate to the directory where the "mnist_nn.py" file is located.

c. Run the script by typing:
python mnist_nn.py

2. View the Results

    a. The script will print the test accuracy to the console.

    b. A plot will appear showing the training and validation accuracy over the epochs.

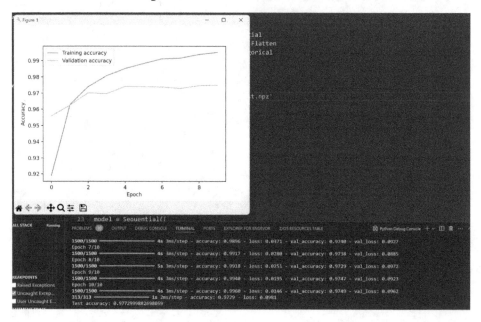

Following these steps enables users to successfully create, train, and evaluate a basic neural network to classify handwritten digits using the MNIST dataset. This exercise provides a practical understanding of how neural networks work and how to implement them using TensorFlow/Keras.

CONCLUSION

This chapter emphasizes the critical role of deep learning in the evolution of AI technologies, underscoring its capacity to tackle increasingly complex challenges. Looking ahead, deep learning is anticipated to further merge with emerging technologies, potentially reducing the need for extensive data and computational resources. This integration aims to make these powerful tools more accessible and efficient, broadening their applicability and enhancing their impact across various sectors.

## CHAPTER 4

NATURAL LANGUAGE PROCESSING (NLP)

Natural Language Processing (NLP) enables machines to understand and interact using human language, forming the basis of applications like virtual assistants, translation services, and sentiment analysis tools. This chapter introduces the fundamental techniques of NLP, from text preprocessing to more complex tasks such as named entity recognition (NER) and machine translation (MT). By exploring the algorithms and methodologfies that underpin NLP, readers will gain insight into how AI can parse, interpret, and generate human language in a way that is both meaningful and impactful. Additionally, the chapter will review the latest advancements in NLP, such as transformers and attention mechanisms, which have significantly enhanced the ability of machines to understand context and semantics. Through practical examples and case studies, this chapter will demonstrate the real-world applications of NLP and its transformative potential across various industries.

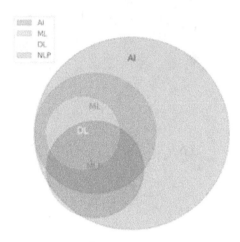

FIGURE 4.1 The relationship between different domains within Artificial Intelligence (AI).

Figure 4.1 illustrates the relationship between different domains within artificial intelligence (AI), with a specific focus on NLP. (*Note: The full color versions of all figures in this text, are available in the companion files.*) The largest circle represents the broad field of AI, which encompasses all forms of intelligent systems and algorithms. Within AI, machine learning (ML) is a subset, depicted by the green circle, which focuses on algorithms that allow systems to learn from data and improve over time. Deep learning (DL), represented by the yellow circle, is a further specialized subset of ML, emphasizing neural networks with many layers that can learn from vast amounts of data. The red circle signifies NLP, which intersects with both ML and DL, highlighting that NLP techniques often rely on these methodologies to process and understand human language. This diagram effectively shows how NLP fits within the broader context of AI, leveraging the advancements in ML and DL to enable machines to interpret, generate, and respond to human language.

INTRODUCTION TO NLP

NLP is a critical domain at the intersection of AI, computer science, and linguistics, aimed at enabling machines to understand and interact with human language. This technology underpins many modern applications such as voice-activated assistants, customer service bots, and automated translation services. NLP faces significant challenges such as deciphering the ambiguities of human language, understanding context, and processing different dialects and slangs. Over the decades, NLP has evolved from rule-based parsing techniques of the 1950s to sophisticated algorithms powered by DL, offering improved accuracy and interaction capabilities in real-world applications.

Fundamentals of NLP

NLP combines computational techniques with linguistic knowledge to enable machines to understand and interact with human language. It encompasses various aspects:

Syntax

Syntax involves the arrangement of words to create meaningful sentences, focusing on the grammatical structure. NLP systems analyze syntactic structures to understand and generate language, ensuring that sentences are both grammatically correct and meaningful. This includes tasks like part-of-speech tagging, parsing, and sentence diagramming. By breaking down sentences into their constituent parts, such as nouns, verbs, adjectives, and adverbs, NLP systems can more accurately interpret the relationships between words. Understanding syntax is crucial for applications like MT, where the correct ordering of words in different languages is essential for accurate communication.

Semantics

Semantics is concerned with interpreting the meanings of sentences, going beyond the syntactic arrangement to understand what the words convey. NLP applies semantic analysis to decode ambiguities in language, ensuring that the intended meaning is captured. This includes tasks like word sense disambiguation, where the meaning of a word is determined based on its context, and semantic role labeling, which identifies the relationship between a verb and its associated nouns. Semantic analysis is crucial for applications like sentiment analysis, where understanding the underlying sentiment of a piece of text depends on accurately interpreting its meaning.

Pragmatics

Pragmatics involves the use of language in social contexts and understanding the intended meaning behind spoken or written communication. It goes beyond literal meaning to consider context, tone, and situational factors that influence interpretation. NLP systems that incorporate pragmatic analysis can better understand idiomatic expressions, sarcasm, and indirect requests. This is essential for applications like virtual assistants, which need to understand not just what is being said, but the context in which it is said, to respond appropriately. Pragmatic analysis helps NLP systems to provide more natural and contextually relevant responses in conversational interfaces.

A historical overview traces NLP's evolution from the early rule-based systems of the 1950s, through the development of statistical models, to today's sophisticated DL techniques.

Techniques in NLP

The following sections describe various preprocessing and analysis techniques that are essential for effective NLP.

Text Preprocessing

Text preprocessing involves several techniques to prepare text for deeper processing in NLP. Tokenization splits text into individual words or phrases, making it easier to analyze. Stemming reduces words to their root form, while lemmatization maps words to their base or dictionary form, both helping in normalizing text. Stop words removal eliminates common words (like "the," "is," "in") that carry little meaning but add noise to the analysis. These preprocessing steps are crucial for enhancing the performance of subsequent NLP tasks by cleaning and structuring the text data, ensuring more accurate and efficient analysis.

Parsing and Part-of-Speech Tagging

Parsing and part-of-speech (POS) tagging are essential for understanding the grammatical structure of a sentence. Parsing determines the hierarchical structure of a sentence, breaking it down into its syntactic components, such as noun phrases and verb phrases. POS tagging assigns parts of speech to each word, such as nouns, verbs, adjectives, and adverbs. This process is crucial for understanding grammatical and logical relationships within the text. Accurate parsing and POS tagging enable more sophisticated NLP tasks, such as semantic analysis, MT, and syntactic error correction, by providing a detailed understanding of sentence structure.

Machine Learning (ML) in NLP

Machine learning (ML) plays a pivotal role in NLP, utilizing algorithms ranging from simple naïve Bayes classifiers to complex neural networks like convolutional neural networks (CNNs) and recurrent neural networks (RNNs). Naïve Bayes is often used for basic tasks like spam detection and sentiment analysis due to its simplicity and efficiency. More complex tasks, such as NER, MT, and question answering, leverage the power of CNNs and RNNs to capture intricate patterns in the data. Advanced models, including transformers, have further enhanced NLP capabilities, enabling more accurate and nuanced understanding and generation of human language across various applications.

Challenges in NLP

NLP faces significant challenges due to the nature of human language. The following sections explore some of those challenges.

Ambiguity and Context

Effective NLP systems must address the inherent ambiguity in language, where meanings can shift dramatically based on context. For instance, the word "bank" can refer to a financial institution or the side of a river, depending on the sentence. Disambiguating such terms requires understanding the surrounding words and the overall context in which they are used. Advanced NLP systems employ techniques such as context-aware embeddings and transformer models to capture these nuances. This ensures more accurate interpretation and generation of language, which is crucial for applications like translation, sentiment analysis, and conversational AI.

Slang and Dialects

Continuously evolving and region-specific slang and dialects present ongoing challenges for NLP systems in understanding and processing everyday language. Slang terms can vary widely even within the same language, reflecting cultural and social dynamics. Dialects add another layer of complexity with unique grammatical structures and vocabulary. To address these challenges, NLP systems must be trained on diverse and up-to-date datasets that include regional variations and informal language. Incorporating user feedback and employing adaptive learning techniques can also help NLP models stay relevant and accurate in the face of rapidly changing linguistic trends.

Resource Availability

There is a scarcity of resources for many languages, which limits the ability to develop robust NLP tools for nonmajor languages. Major languages like English, Spanish, and Chinese benefit from extensive datasets, pretrained models, and research focus. In contrast, many languages lack sufficient annotated data, linguistic research, and computational resources, making it difficult to build effective NLP applications. Efforts to create multilingual datasets, transfer learning techniques, and community-driven initiatives are essential to bridge this gap. Enhancing resource availability for underrepresented languages is crucial for making NLP technology accessible and beneficial to a broader global audience.

Real-World Applications of NLP

NLP has a wide range of applications that demonstrate its versatility. The following sections describe some of those applications.

Voice-Activated Assistants

Systems like Amazon Echo and Google Home demonstrate advanced speech recognition and understanding, enabling interaction through voice commands. These devices use NLP to process and interpret spoken language, allowing users to perform tasks such as setting reminders, playing music, controlling smart home devices, and retrieving information through simple voice interactions. The integration of ML algorithms helps these assistants continuously improve their accuracy and responsiveness, adapting to users' speech patterns and preferences over time. This seamless voice interaction enhances user convenience and accessibility, making technology more intuitive and integrated into daily life.

Customer Service Bots

NLP-driven chatbots efficiently manage customer queries, providing responses and support based on the understanding of user inputs. These bots are deployed across various platforms, including Web sites, messaging apps, and customer service portals, to assist users with tasks like troubleshooting, booking appointments, and answering frequently asked questions. By leveraging NLP, chatbots can understand context, sentiment, and intent, enabling them to provide relevant and timely assistance. This automation not only improves customer satisfaction by offering instant support but also reduces the workload on human agents, allowing them to focus on more complex issues.

Automated Translation Services

Tools such as Google Translate leverage NLP for translating text and speech between multiple languages, facilitating global communication. These services use advanced algorithms to understand the context and nuances of the source language, producing more accurate and fluent translations. By incorporating DL models, such as neural MT, these tools can manage complex sentence structures and idiomatic expressions, providing high-quality translations. Automated translation services enable individuals and businesses to communicate effectively across language barriers, supporting international collaboration, education, and travel. They also continue to improve through user feedback and ongoing advancements in NLP research.

TEXT PREPROCESSING

Text preprocessing is a foundational step in NLP that prepares raw text data for further analysis and processing. This involves several techniques that are explained in the following sections.

Tokenization

Tokenization splits text into sentences or words, forming the first step in text preprocessing for NLP. This process involves breaking down a string of text into smaller, manageable pieces called tokens. Tokens can be individual words, phrases, or even whole sentences, depending on the application. Proper tokenization is crucial as it affects the accuracy of subsequent NLP tasks like parsing, NER, and sentiment analysis. Advanced tokenization methods consider language-specific nuances, punctuation, and special characters, ensuring that the text is segmented in a way that retains its meaningful structure for analysis.

Stemming

Stemming reduces words to their base or root form, typically by removing suffixes and prefixes. This process helps in normalizing the text, allowing NLP systems to treat different forms of a word (e.g., "running," "runner," "runs") as a single entity, thereby improving the performance of information retrieval and text analysis tasks. Although stemming can sometimes produce nondictionary words, its simplicity and efficiency make it useful for applications where speed and broad coverage are more important than linguistic accuracy. For instance, search engines often use stemming to improve search results by matching queries with relevant documents.

Lemmatization

Lemmatization like stemming, involves cutting words down to their lemma or dictionary form, but with a more sophisticated approach. It considers the morphological analysis of the words, using vocabulary and context to determine the correct base form (e.g., "better" to "good" and "running" to "run"). Lemmatization ensures that the resulting words are valid and meaningful, which enhances the accuracy of NLP tasks like POS tagging and MT. This process requires more computational resources than stemming but provides better linguistic accuracy, making it ideal for applications where precise text analysis is critical.

Removing Stop Words

Removing stop words eliminates common words that add little value in the context of data analysis. Words such as "and" "the," "is," and "in" are frequently removed from text data to reduce noise and improve the efficiency of NLP algorithms. These words are often ubiquitous and do not contribute significantly to the meaning of the text, thus their removal helps in focusing on more important terms that carry substantial information. This step is particularly useful in tasks like text classification, sentiment analysis, and keyword extraction, where the goal is to identify and analyze the core content of the text.

These techniques help in normalizing text and are essential for effective feature extraction in later stages of NLP workflows. Tools like NLTK, spaCy, and textblob provide extensive support for these preprocessing tasks, enabling developers to implement them efficiently.

SENTIMENT ANALYSIS

Sentiment analysis is the computational study of people's opinions, sentiments, attitudes, and emotions expressed in written language. It is widely used in analyzing customer feedback, social media monitoring, and brand management. Techniques range from simple rule-based algorithms that scan for positive and negative words, to complex ML models that can understand nuances in emotional context. Recent advancements involve using DL architectures like long short-term memory (LSTM) and transformers that can analyze the sentiment context better due to their ability to understand sequence and context in text data. These models can handle the subtleties of sarcasm, irony, and varying tones of voice, providing more accurate sentiment insights. Additionally, sentiment analysis is being applied to voice data in customer service interactions to gauge caller satisfaction, and in financial markets to predict stock movements based on public sentiment. The continuous improvement in NLP techniques ensures that sentiment analysis becomes increasingly dependable and integral to strategic decision-making across industries.

FIGURE 4.2 The concept of sentiment analysis.

Figure 4.2 illustrates the concept of sentiment analysis, which involves determining the emotional tone behind a series of words to gain an understanding of the attitudes, opinions, and emotions expressed within an online mention. (*Note: The full color versions of all figures in this text, are available in the companion files.*) The green circle with a smiling face represents a positive sentiment, indicating contentment or happiness. The red circle with a sad face signifies a negative sentiment, reflecting dissatisfaction or unhappiness. The yellow circle with a neutral face denotes a neutral sentiment, where the emotion expressed is neither particularly positive nor negative. Sentiment analysis algorithms process text data to classify these emotions, providing valuable insights for applications such as customer feedback analysis, market research, and social media monitoring.

NAMED ENTITY RECOGNITION

Named entity recognition (NER) is a process where the machine reads a text and identifies entities mentioned in the text such as names of people, companies, locations, dates, and other proper nouns. This is crucial for structuring and categorizing unstructured data for tasks such as information retrieval, automated customer support, and content classification. NER systems typically use two approaches: rule-based, which relies on predefined patterns and dictionaries, and statistical, which includes ML models like conditional random fields (CRFs) and neural networks. Tools such as Stanford NER and spaCy offer prebuilt NER capabilities which can be customized and trained on domain-specific datasets. Recent advancements also incorporate DL models like BERT and transformers, enhancing the accuracy and adaptability of NER systems by better understanding the context and subtleties in language. These improvements make NER an essential component in applications like news summarization, bioinformatics, and legal document analysis, where accurate identification and classification of entities are critical.

MACHINE TRANSLATION

Machine translation (MT) is the task of automatically converting text from one language to another. From early rule-based systems to the latest neural machine translation (NMT) models, MT has significantly advanced the removal of language barriers in global communication. NMT, which uses DL-based models such as sequence-to-sequence (seq2seq) architectures, has improved the quality of translation by considering the entire input sentence and maintaining context across sentences. Moreover, the introduction of transformer-based models like Google's BERT and OpenAI's GPT has further enhanced translation accuracy by capturing complex linguistic patterns and nuances. Despite these advancements, challenges still exist in dealing with idiomatic expressions, cultural nuances, and maintaining the quality across various language pairs. Additionally, translating low-resource languages, which lack extensive training data, remains a significant hurdle. Continuous research and development in NMT aim to address these challenges, making MT systems more robust and capable of delivering high-quality translations across a broader spectrum of languages and contexts.

AI APPLICATION: PERFORM SENTIMENT ANALYSIS ON A SET OF MOVIE REVIEWS

In this AI Application, users will perform sentiment analysis on a set of movie reviews using Python, NLTK, and Scikit-learn. This guide provides step-by-step instructions to preprocess text data, train a sentiment analysis model, and evaluate its performance, including:

- *Step 1*: Set Up Development Environment

- *Step 2*: Load and Preprocess the Dataset

- *Step 3*: Train the Sentiment Analysis Model

- *Step 4*: Evaluate the Model

- *Step 5*: Run the Script

Step 1: Set Up Development Environment

1. Install Python

   a. Follow the instructions in the previous examples to download and install Python.

2. Install Necessary Libraries

   a. Open a terminal or command prompt.
   b. Install the required libraries by typing:
   pip install nltk scikit-learn pandas

3. Download NLTK Data

   a. Open a Python shell or script.
   b. Download the necessary NLTK data:
   import nltk
   nltk.download('punkt')
   nltk.download('stopwords')\
   nltk.download('movie_reviews')

Step 2: Load and Preprocess the Movie Reviews Dataset

1. Open the Code Editor

    a. Use preferred text editor or IDE.

2. Create a New Python File

    a. Create a new file named "sentiment_analysis.py."

3. Import Necessary Libraries

    a. At the top of the "sentiment_analysis.py" file, import the necessary libraries.

```python
1   import nltk
2
3   from nltk.corpus import movie_reviews, stopwords
4   from sklearn.feature_extraction.text import CountVectorizer
5   from sklearn.model_selection import train_test_split
6   from sklearn.naive_bayes import MultinomialNB
7   from sklearn.metrics import accuracy_score, classification_report
8   import pandas as pd
```

4. Load the Movie Reviews Dataset

    a. Load the dataset and create a DataFrame.

```python
# Load the movie reviews dataset
def load_data():
    reviews = [(list(movie_reviews.words(fileid)), category)
                for category in movie_reviews.categories()
                for fileid in movie_reviews.fileids(category)]
    return reviews

reviews = load_data()
```

5. Preprocess the Data

    a. Define a function to preprocess the text data.

```python
23   # Preprocess the data
24   def preprocess_text(words):
25       stop_words = set(stopwords.words('english'))
26       words_filtered = [word.lower() for word in words if word.isalpha() and word.lower() not in stop_words]
27       return ' '.join(words_filtered)
28
29   reviews_processed = [(preprocess_text(words), category) for words, category in reviews]
30   df = pd.DataFrame(reviews_processed, columns=['review', 'sentiment'])
```

Step 3: Train the Sentiment Analysis Model

1. Split the Data into Training and Testing Sets

   a. Split the data into input features (X) and target variable (Y), then into training and testing sets.

```
32  # Split the data into training and testing sets
33  X = df['review']
34  Y = df['sentiment']
35  X_train, X_test, Y_train, Y_test = train_test_split(X, Y, test_size=0.2, random_state=42)
```

2. Vectorize the Text Data

   a. Convert the text data into numerical features using CountVectorizer.

```
37  # Vectorize the text data
38  vectorizer = CountVectorizer()
39  X_train_vectorized = vectorizer.fit_transform(X_train)
40  X_test_vectorized = vectorizer.transform(X_test)
```

3. Train the Model

   a. Create and train a naïve Bayes classifier.

```
42  # Train          Naive Bayes classifier for multinomia
43  model = MultinomialNB()
44  model.fit(X_train_vectorized, Y_train)
45
46  # Make predictions
```

Step 4: Evaluate the Model

1. Make Predictions

   a. Make predictions on the test data.

2. Evaluate the Model

   a. Calculate and print the accuracy score and classification report.

```
49  # Evaluate the model
50  accuracy = accuracy_score(Y_test, Y_pred)
51  print(f"Accuracy: {accuracy}")
52  print("Classification Report:")
53  print(classification_report(Y_test, Y_pred))
```

3. Complete Script

a. The complete "sentiment_analysis.py" file should look as follows:

```python
import nltk

from nltk.corpus import movie_reviews, stopwords
from sklearn.feature_extraction.text import CountVectorizer
from sklearn.model_selection import train_test_split
from sklearn.naive_bayes import MultinomialNB
from sklearn.metrics import accuracy_score, classification_report
import pandas as pd

# Download necessary NLTK data
nltk.download('stopwords')
nltk.download('movie_reviews')

# Load the movie reviews dataset
def load_data():
    reviews = [(list(movie_reviews.words(fileid)), category)
               for category in movie_reviews.categories()
               for fileid in movie_reviews.fileids(category)]
    return reviews

reviews = load_data()

# Preprocess the data
def preprocess_text(words):
    stop_words = set(stopwords.words('english'))
    words_filtered = [word.lower() for word in words if word.isalpha() and word.lower() not in stop_words]
    return ' '.join(words_filtered)

reviews_processed = [(preprocess_text(words), category) for words, category in reviews]
df = pd.DataFrame(reviews_processed, columns=['review', 'sentiment'])

# Split the data into training and testing sets
X = df['review']
Y = df['sentiment']
X_train, X_test, Y_train, Y_test = train_test_split(X, Y, test_size=0.2, random_state=42)

# Vectorize the text data
vectorizer = CountVectorizer()
X_train_vectorized = vectorizer.fit_transform(X_train)
X_test_vectorized = vectorizer.transform(X_test)

# Train the model
model = MultinomialNB()
model.fit(X_train_vectorized, Y_train)

# Make predictions
Y_pred = model.predict(X_test_vectorized)

# Evaluate the model
accuracy = accuracy_score(Y_test, Y_pred)
print(f"Accuracy: {accuracy}")
print("Classification Report:")
print(classification_report(Y_test, Y_pred))
```

Step 5: Run the Script

1. Run the Script

   a. Open a terminal or command prompt.

   b. Navigate to the directory where the "sentiment_analysis.py" file is located.

   c. Run the script by typing:
   python sentiment_analysis.py

2. View the Results

   a. The script will print the accuracy score and classification report to the console.

```
sentiment_analysis.py > ...
 1   import nltk
 2
 3   from nltk.corpus import movie_reviews, stopwords
 4   from sklearn.feature_extraction.text import CountVectorizer
 5   from sklearn.model_selection import train_test_split
 6   from sklearn.naive_bayes import MultinomialNB
 7   from sklearn.metrics import accuracy_score, classification_report
 8   import pandas as pd
 9
10   # Download necessary NLTK data
11   nltk.download('stopwords')
12   nltk.download('movie_reviews')
13
14   # Load the movie reviews dataset
15   def load_data():
16       reviews = [(list(movie_reviews.words(fileid)), category)
17                   for category in movie_reviews.categories()
18                   for fileid in movie_reviews.fileids(category)]
19       return reviews
20
21   reviews = load_data()
22
```

```
PROBLEMS  14    OUTPUT    DEBUG CONSOLE    TERMINAL    PORTS    EXPLORER FOR ENDEVOR    Z/OS RESOURCES TABLE

Accuracy: 0.8125
Classification Report:
              precision    recall   f1-score   support

         neg      0.79      0.85       0.82       199
         pos      0.84      0.77       0.81       201

    accuracy                          0.81       400
   macro avg      0.81      0.81       0.81       400
weighted avg      0.81      0.81       0.81       400
```

Following these steps enables users to successfully perform sentiment analysis on a set of movie reviews using Python, NLTK, and Scikit-learn. This exercise demonstrates the process of text preprocessing, model training, and evaluation, providing a practical understanding of how sentiment analysis works in NLP.

CONCLUSION

NLP continues to be a dynamic field within AI, pushing the boundaries of how machines understand human language. The development of advanced techniques in DL and the increasing availability of big data are driving innovations that enhance the accuracy and applicability of NLP applications. Future directions might include more sophisticated contextual understanding, real-time multilanguage translation, and further integration of NLP into everyday devices to make interactions more natural and intuitive.

## CHAPTER 5

COMPUTER VISION

omputer vision is an AI field that trains computers to interpret and understand the visual world. This chapter covers the fundamental concepts of image processing and defines advanced topics such as object detection, image classification, and image segmentation. Each section includes practical applications that highlight how computer vision is transforming industries by enabling machines to perform tasks traditionally requiring human visual comprehension, such as medical imaging analysis and autonomous vehicle navigation. Additionally, the chapter examines the latest advancements in computer vision, including the use of convolutional neural networks (CNNs) and deep learning techniques that significantly enhance the accuracy and efficiency of visual recognition systems. Real-world examples and case studies illustrate the powerful impact of computer vision in diverse areas such as security surveillance, facial recognition, augmented reality, and manufacturing quality control, highlighting the extensive potential of this technology in revolutionizing various sectors.

INTRODUCTION TO COMPUTER VISION

Computer vision is an artificial intelligence discipline that enables computers to interpret and make sense of the visual world. Machines analyze visual information the way humans do but use cameras, data, and algorithms instead of eyes and brains. This field has expanded dramatically with the advent of deep learning, improving the capabilities of systems in recognizing and interpreting images and videos. From early image processing to advanced AI-driven analytics, computer vision is pivotal in numerous applications, such as facial recognition, automated inspection, and augmented reality. These advancements have led to significant improvements in industries like healthcare, where computer vision aids in diagnosing diseases through medical imaging, and in automotive sectors, where it supports the development of autonomous driving technologies. Moreover, the integration of computer vision with other AI technologies continues to open new possibilities for innovation, making it a cornerstone of modern technological advancements.

IMAGE PREPROCESSING

Image preprocessing is a crucial first step in computer vision, aimed at improving image data by suppressing unwanted distortions and enhancing image features important for further processing. Some techniques are discussed in the following sections.

Grayscale Conversion

Grayscale conversion simplifies images by reducing them to shades of gray, which simplifies the analysis by eliminating the influence of color. This process transforms a colorful image into one that only contains variations in brightness, making it easier to focus on structural and textural features. Grayscale images are computationally less intensive to process and are often used in preprocessing steps for various computer vision tasks such as object detection and face recognition, where color information is less critical than shape and intensity patterns.

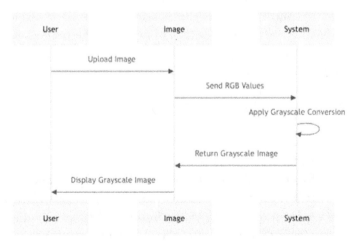

FIGURE 5.1 The sequence of steps involved in converting an RGB image to grayscale.

Figure 5.1 illustrates the sequence of steps involved in converting an RGB image to grayscale. The process begins with the user uploading an image, followed by the image sending its RGB values to the system. The system then applies the grayscale conversion algorithm and returns the processed grayscale image to the original image. Finally, the image displays the grayscale version to the user.

Histogram Equalization

Histogram equalization enhances the contrast of an image to allow for better feature extraction. This technique redistributes the intensity values of the image so that they span the entire range of values, making features more distinguishable. By improving the visibility of edges and details in both bright and dark areas, histogram equalization can significantly enhance the performance of computer vision algorithms, especially in scenarios where lighting conditions vary, such as in medical imaging or remote sensing.

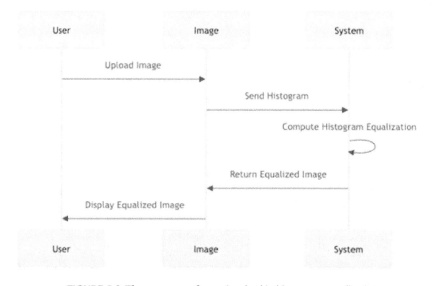

FIGURE 5.2 The sequence of steps involved in histogram equalization.

Figure 5.2 illustrates the sequence of steps involved in histogram equalization. The process starts with the user uploading an image, followed by the image sending its histogram to the system. The system computes the histogram equalization and returns the equalized image back to the original image. Finally, the image displays the equalized version to the user.

Normalization

Normalization scales pixel values to a standard range, such as [0, 1] or [-1, 1], to improve the stability and performance of learning algorithms. This process ensures that all input data contributes equally to the model, preventing any single feature from disproportionately affecting the outcome. Normalization helps in accelerating the convergence of gradient descent algorithms, leading to faster and more reliable training of machine learning models. It is particularly important in deep learning, where consistent input ranges can significantly impact the performance of neural networks.

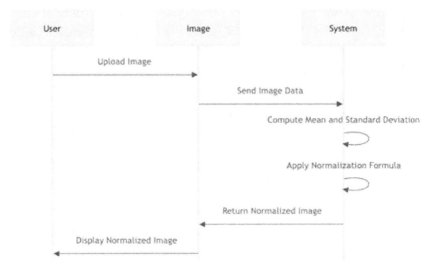

FIGURE 5.3 The sequence of steps involved in normalization.

Edge Detection

Edge detection identifies the boundaries of objects within an image, which is crucial for object localization and shape detection. Techniques like the Canny, Sobel, and Prewitt operators are used to detect sharp changes in intensity, indicating the presence of edges. Edge detection is a fundamental step in image processing pipelines, enabling applications such as image segmentation, pattern recognition, and computer vision tasks like face detection and lane detection in autonomous driving. By highlighting the structural contours of objects, edge detection facilitates accurate analysis and interpretation of visual data.

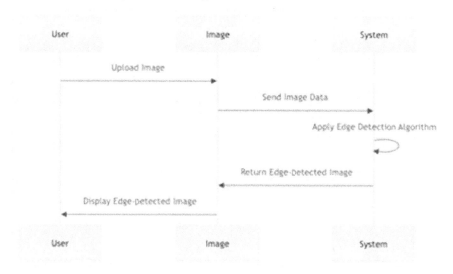

FIGURE 5.4 The sequence of steps involved in edge detection.

Figure 5.4 illustrates the sequence of steps involved in edge detection. The process starts with the user uploading an image, followed by the image sending its data to the system. The system applies the edge detection algorithm and returns the edge-detected image back to the original image. Finally, the image displays the edge-detected version to the user.

Tools such as OpenCV provide comprehensive functions that support these preprocessing steps, making them essential in building efficient computer vision models.

OBJECT DETECTION

Object detection is fundamental in computer vision, designed to identify and locate objects within an image or video. This task goes beyond classification by not only categorizing the objects presented in an image but also indicating their specific location and scale within the scene.

FIGURE 5.5 A representation of object detection in computer vision.

Figure 5.5 represents object detection in computer vision. It shows a computer screen with various objects highlighted by bounding boxes and labels, alongside the relevant code. Key techniques like classification, localization, bounding boxes, and scale are also included.

Some techniques are described in the following sections.

Region-Based Convolutional Neural Networks (R-CNNs)

Region-based convolutional neural networks (R-CNNs) revolutionized object detection by using regional proposals to locate objects within an image. The original R-CNN algorithm selects numerous region proposals and runs a CNN on each, which is computationally intensive. To address this, Faster R-CNN and Fast R-CNN were developed. Fast R-CNN improves speed by sharing convolutional layers across proposals, while Faster R-CNN further enhances efficiency with a region proposal network (RPN) that generates proposals in real-time. These advancements significantly reduce processing time while improving detection accuracy, making them highly effective for applications like object recognition in images and video analysis.

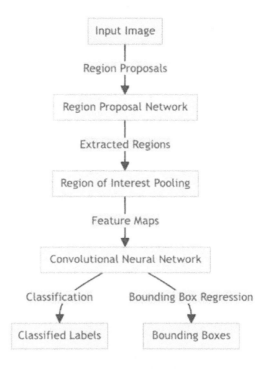

FIGURE 5.6 The structure and workflow of R-CNNs.

Figure 5.6 illustrates the structure and workflow of R-CNNs. The process starts with an input image which is processed by the region proposal network (RPN) to generate region proposals. These proposals are then subjected to region of interest (ROI) pooling to extract relevant feature maps. The feature maps are further processed by a CNN to perform classification, resulting in classified labels and bounding box regression, which produces bounding boxes for the detected objects.

YOLO (You Only Look Once)

YOLO (You Only Look Once) is renowned for its speed and efficiency in detecting objects in real-time. Unlike traditional methods that use a pipeline of separate stages, YOLO treats object detection as a single regression problem, predicting bounding boxes and class probabilities directly from full images in one evaluation. This approach allows YOLO to achieve high frame rates, making it ideal for real-time applications such as autonomous driving, security surveillance, and live video analytics. YOLO's ability to process images quickly without compromising accuracy makes it a popular choice for time-sensitive detection tasks.

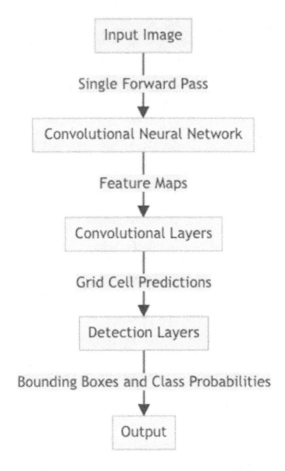

FIGURE 5.7 The structure and workflow of YOLO (You Only Look Once).

Figure 5.7 illustrates the structure and workflow of YOLO (You Only Look Once). The process begins with an input image that undergoes a single forward pass through a CNN. The CNN generates feature maps, which are then processed by convolutional layers. These layers make predictions for each grid cell in the image, which are passed to the detection layers. The detection layers output bounding boxes and class probabilities, which are combined to produce the final detection results.

SSD (Single Shot Multidetector)

SSD (single shot multidetector) balances speed and accuracy by detecting objects in a single shot. SSD improves upon previous methods by using a single neural network that predicts bounding boxes and class scores for multiple objects at different scales, directly from feature maps. This eliminates the need for regional proposal steps, significantly speeding up the detection process. SSD's architecture allows it to perform well on real-time applications, including mobile and embedded systems, where both computational resources and detection accuracy are critical. Its efficient yet accurate object detection capabilities make it suitable for a wide range of practical uses, from robotics to augmented reality.

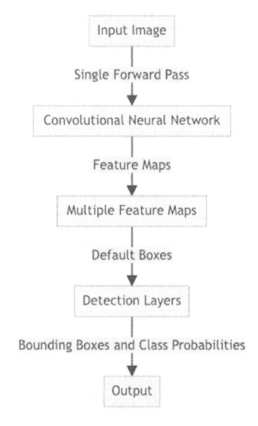

FIGURE 5.8 The structure and workflow of SSD (single shot multidetector)

Figure 5.8 illustrates the structure and workflow of SSD (single shot multidetector). The process starts with an input image that undergoes a single forward pass through a CNN. The CNN generates multiple feature maps at different scales, which are then used to create default boxes. These default boxes are processed by detection layers to produce bounding boxes and class probabilities, resulting in the final detection outputs.

Applications range from security (detecting unauthorized individuals) to autonomous vehicles (identifying pedestrians or other vehicles), highlighting the adaptability and necessity of object detection in modern technology.

IMAGE CLASSIFICATION

Image classification involves categorizing and labeling groups of pixels within an image into various classes. This task is fundamental in computer vision, with applications spanning numerous fields:

Convolutional Neural Networks (CNNs)

Convolutional neural networks (CNNs) are used due to their high accuracy in recognizing visual patterns. They excel in tasks such as image classification, object detection, and image segmentation by leveraging convolutional layers that automatically and hierarchically detect features like edges, textures, and more complex shapes. CNNs have transformed computer vision, enabling applications like facial recognition, medical image analysis, and autonomous driving. Their architecture, which includes layers like convolutional, pooling, and fully connected layers, allows CNNs to learn and generalize from visual data effectively, making them indispensable for modern image and video analysis tasks.

Machine Learning Algorithms

Machine learning algorithms such as support vector machines (SVMs) and random forests are also employed, especially where training data is limited. SVMs are effective for classification tasks by finding the optimal hyperplane that separates data points into distinct categories. Random forests, which use an ensemble of decision trees, are robust for both classification and regression tasks, offering high accuracy and resistance to overfitting. These traditional algorithms are valuable in scenarios where deep learning might be impractical due to smaller datasets or limited computational resources. Their simplicity and effectiveness make them suitable for applications like fraud detection, market analysis, and bioinformatics.

In practice, image classification is used to categorize medical imagery, organize large databases of digital media, and enable retail systems to categorize products automatically.

IMAGE SEGMENTATION

Image segmentation partitions an image into multiple segments to simplify and change the representation of an image into something more meaningful and easier to analyze. It is a critical process in medical imaging for identifying regions of interest, in autonomous driving to understand and navigate the road, and in agricultural technology to monitor crop health from aerial images. Some techniques of image segmentation are described in the following sections.

Thresholding

Thresholding is the simplest method of image segmentation that involves segmenting based on pixel intensity values. By setting a threshold value, pixels are divided into different classes; for example, all pixels with intensity above the threshold might be assigned to one class and the rest to another. This technique is particularly effective for images with sharp contrast between the objects and the background, such as in document image binarization. Despite its simplicity, thresholding can be immensely powerful in applications like detecting defects in industrial inspection or isolating features in remote sensing images.

Clustering Methods

Clustering methods, such as k-means, group pixels into clusters based on feature similarities. K-means clustering iteratively assigns pixels to k clusters by minimizing the variance within each cluster, effectively segmenting the image into regions with similar characteristics. This method is useful for images where distinct regions can be identified by color, texture, or intensity. Clustering methods are widely used in applications like image compression, where they reduce the color palette, and in medical imaging, where they help in segmenting different tissues or detecting abnormalities in scans.

Advanced Methods

Advanced methods, such as watershed segmentation, are used for more complex scenarios like medical image analysis. The watershed algorithm treats the grayscale image as a topographic surface, where high-intensity values represent peaks and low-intensity values represent valleys. The algorithm then "floods" the valleys, segmenting the image into distinct regions. This method is particularly effective for separating touching or overlapping objects in an image. In medical imaging, watershed segmentation can help delineate structures like cells or organs, facilitating accurate diagnosis and treatment planning. Advanced methods are crucial in scenarios requiring precise and detailed image analysis.

AI APPLICATION: IMPLEMENT AN IMAGE CLASSIFICATION MODEL USING CIFAR-10 DATASET

In this AI application, users will implement an image classification model using the CIFAR-10 dataset. This guide provides step-by-step instructions for image preprocessing, model building, training, and evaluation using Python, TensorFlow/Keras, and OpenCV, including:

- *Step 1*: Set Up Development Environment

- *Step 2*: Load and Preprocess the CIFAR-10 Dataset

- *Step 3*: Build the Image Classification Model

- *Step 4*: Train the Image Classification Model

- *Step 5*: Evaluate the Model

- *Step 6*: Run the Script

Step 1: Set Up Development Environment

1. Install Python:

   a. Follow the instructions in the previous examples to download and install Python.

2. Install Necessary Libraries:

   b. Open a terminal or command prompt.
   c. Install the required libraries by typing:
   pip install tensorflow opencv-python

Step 2: Load and Preprocess the CIFAR-10 Dataset

1. Open the Code Editor:

   - Use preferred text editor or IDE.

2. Create a New Python File:

   - Create a new file named "cifar10_classification.py."

3. Import Necessary Libraries:

- At the top of the "cifar10_classification.py" file, import the necessary libraries:

```
1   import tensorflow as tf
2   from tensorflow.keras.datasets import cifar10
3   from tensorflow.keras.models import Sequential
4   from tensorflow.keras.layers import Dense, Conv2D, MaxPooling2D, Flatten, Dropout
5   from tensorflow.keras.utils import to_categorical
6   import matplotlib.pyplot as plt
7   import os
```

4. Load the CIFAR-10 Dataset:

- Load the dataset and split it into training and testing sets.

```
9    # Path to the locally downloaded CIFAR-10 dataset
10   local_path = '/Users/erikherman/Documents/GitHub/PublicInformationLimited/AI_Revealed/cifar-10-batches-py'
11
12   def load_local_cifar10(path):
13       import pickle
14       import numpy as np
15
16       def load_batch(fpath):
17           with open(fpath, 'rb') as f:
18               d = pickle.load(f, encoding='bytes')
19               d_decoded = {k.decode('utf8'): v for k, v in d.items()}
20           data = d_decoded['data']
21           labels = d_decoded['labels']
22           data = data.reshape(data.shape[0], 3, 32, 32)
23           return data, labels
24
25       num_train_samples = 50000
26       x_train = np.empty((num_train_samples, 3, 32, 32), dtype='uint8')
27       y_train = np.empty((num_train_samples,), dtype='uint8')
```

5. Preprocess the Data:

- Convert the labels to one-hot encoded vectors.

```
49   # Preprocess the data
50   X_train = X_train.astype('float32') / 255
51   X_test = X_test.astype('float32') / 255
52   Y_train = to_categorical(Y_train, 10)
53   Y_test = to_categorical(Y_test, 10)
```

Step 3: Build the Image Classification Model

1. Create the Model:

   • Build a sequential model and add layers:

```
55  # Build the model
56  model = Sequential([
57      Conv2D(32, (3, 3), activation='relu', input_shape=(32, 32, 3)),
58      MaxPooling2D((2, 2)),
59      Conv2D(64, (3, 3), activation='relu'),
60      MaxPooling2D((2, 2)),
61      Conv2D(128, (3, 3), activation='relu'),
62      Flatten(),
63      Dense(128, activation='relu'),
64      Dropout(0.5),
65      Dense(10, activation='softmax')
66  ])
```

2. Compile the Model:

   • Compile the model with an appropriate optimizer, loss function, and metrics:

```
68  # Compile the model
69  model.compile(optimizer='adam', loss='categorical_crossentropy', metrics=['accuracy'])
```

Step 4: Train the Image Classification Model

1. Train the Model:

   • Train the model on the training data.

```
71  # Train the model
72  history = model.fit(X_train, Y_train, epochs=20, validation_split=0.2, batch_size=64)
```

Step 5: Evaluate the Model

1. Evaluate the Model:

   • Evaluate the model on the test data.

```
74  # Evaluate the model
75  test_loss, test_accuracy = model.evaluate(X_test, Y_test)
76  print(f"Test accuracy: {test_accuracy}")
```

2. Visualize Training History:

- Plot the training and validation accuracy over epochs.

```
78  # Visualize training history
79  plt.plot(history.history['accuracy'], label='Training accuracy')
80  plt.plot(history.history['val_accuracy'], label='Validation accuracy')
81  plt.xlabel('Epoch')
82  plt.ylabel('Accuracy')
83  plt.legend()
84  plt.show()
```

3. Get Predictions.

```
90  # Get predictions
91  predictions = model.predict(X_test)
92  predicted_classes = np.argmax(predictions, axis=1)
93  true_classes = np.argmax(Y_test, axis=1)
```

4. Complete Script:

- The complete "cifar10_classification.py" file should look like this:

```
import matplotlib.pyplot as plt
import numpy as np
import tensorflow as tf
from tensorflow.keras.datasets import cifar10
from tensorflow.keras.models import Sequential
from tensorflow.keras.layers import Dense, Conv2D,
MaxPooling2D, Flatten, Dropout
from tensorflow.keras.utils import to_categorical
import matplotlib.pyplot as plt
import os

# Path to the locally downloaded CIFAR-10 dataset
local_path = '/Users/erikherman/Documents/GitHub/
PublicInformationLimited/AI_Revealed/cifar-10-batches-py'

def load_local_cifar10(path):
import pickle
import numpy as np
```

```python
def load_batch(fpath):
with open(fpath, 'rb') as f:
d = pickle.load(f, encoding='bytes')
d_decoded = {k.decode('utf8'): v for k, v in d.items()}
data = d_decoded['data']
labels = d_decoded['labels']
data = data.reshape(data.shape[0], 3, 32, 32)
return data, labels

num_train_samples = 50000
x_train = np.empty((num_train_samples, 3, 32, 32),
dtype='uint8')
y_train = np.empty((num_train_samples,), dtype='uint8')

for i in range(1, 6):
fpath = os.path.join(path, 'data_batch_' + str(i))
data, labels = load_batch(fpath)
x_train[(i - 1) * 10000: i * 10000, :, :, :] = data
y_train[(i - 1) * 10000: i * 10000] = labels

fpath = os.path.join(path, 'test_batch')
x_test, y_test = load_batch(fpath)

y_train = np.reshape(y_train, (len(y_train), 1))
y_test = np.reshape(y_test, (len(y_test), 1))

x_train = x_train.transpose(0, 2, 3, 1)
x_test = x_test.transpose(0, 2, 3, 1)

return (x_train, y_train), (x_test, y_test)

# Load the CIFAR-10 dataset from the local path
(X_train, Y_train), (X_test, Y_test) = load_local_cifar10(local_path)

# Preprocess the data
X_train = X_train.astype('float32') / 255
X_test = X_test.astype('float32') / 255
Y_train = to_categorical(Y_train, 10)
Y_test = to_categorical(Y_test, 10)
```

```python
# Build the model
model = Sequential([
Conv2D(32, (3, 3), activation='relu', input_shape=(32, 32, 3)),
MaxPooling2D((2, 2)),
Conv2D(64, (3, 3), activation='relu'),
MaxPooling2D((2, 2)),
Conv2D(128, (3, 3), activation='relu'),
Flatten(),
Dense(128, activation='relu'),
Dropout(0.5),
Dense(10, activation='softmax')
])

# Compile the model
model.compile(optimizer='adam', loss='categorical_
crossentropy', metrics=['accuracy'])

# Train the model
history = model.fit(X_train, Y_train, epochs=20, validation_
split=0.2, batch_size=64)

# Evaluate the model
test_loss, test_accuracy = model.evaluate(X_test, Y_test)
print(f"Test accuracy: {test_accuracy}")

# Visualize training history
plt.plot(history.history['accuracy'], label='Training accuracy')
plt.plot(history.history['val_accuracy'], label='Validation
accuracy')
plt.xlabel('Epoch')
plt.ylabel('Accuracy')
plt.legend()
plt.show()

# Assuming X_test, Y_test, and model are already defined

# Get predictions
predictions = model.predict(X_test)
predicted_classes = np.argmax(predictions, axis=1)
true_classes = np.argmax(Y_test, axis=1)
```

```
# Function to plot images and labels
def plot_images(images, true_labels, predicted_labels):
plt.figure(figsize=(10, 5))
for i in range(10):
plt.subplot(2, 5, i+1)
plt.imshow(images[i])
plt.xticks([])
plt.yticks([])
plt.title(f"True: {true_labels[i]}\nPred: {predicted_labels[i]}")
plt.show()

# Select a subset of images
plot_images(X_test[:10], true_classes[:10], predicted_classes[:10])
```

Step 6: Run the Script

1. Run the Script:

    • Open a terminal or command prompt.

    Navigate to the directory where the "cifar10_classification.py" file is locatRun the script by typing:

    ```
    python cifar10_classification.py
    ```

2. View the Results:

    • The script will print the test accuracy to the console.

    • A plot will appear showing the training and validation accuracy over the epochs.

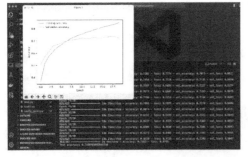
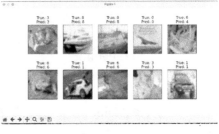

Following these steps enables users to successfully implement an image classification model using the CIFAR-10 dataset. This exercise demonstrates the process of image preprocessing, model building, training, and evaluation, providing a practical understanding of how to work with image data in computer vision tasks using TensorFlow/Keras.

CONCLUSION

Computer vision fundamentally transforms how machines interact with the visual world, bridging the gap between digital data and human-like understanding. Its development heralds significant advancements in technology, making processes more efficient, accurate, and cost-effective. Future trends may include enhanced real-time processing capabilities, deeper integration with other branches of AI, and expanded use of unsupervised learning methods to manage increasingly complex tasks in computer vision.

This comprehensive exploration into computer vision equips readers with a deep understanding of both its foundational elements and innovative applications, illustrating the profound impact it continues to have across diverse industries.

## CHAPTER 6

ETHICS AND BIAS IN AI

A I technology is not just a technical endeavor but also an ethical one. This chapter addresses the critical issues of ethics and bias in AI, discussing the moral implications of automated decision-making and the challenges of ensuring fairness, accountability, and transparency in AI systems. As AI becomes more integrated into everyday life, the potential for unintended consequences and discriminatory practices increases, necessitating robust ethical frameworks. This chapter also explores the landscape of AI regulation and governance, offering insights into how different countries and organizations are approaching these pressing issues. Readers will examine case studies that highlight both the successes and failures in managing ethical considerations in AI, providing a comprehensive understanding of the current state and future direction of AI ethics. This chapter serves as a call to action for responsible AI development and deployment, emphasizing the importance of interdisciplinary collaboration to create AI systems that are beneficial and equitable for all members of society.

FIGURE 6.1 Delicate equilibrium between human cognition, technological advancements, and ethical considerations.

ETHICAL CONSIDERATIONS IN AI

Artificial intelligence brings forth profound ethical challenges that influence societal norms and individual rights. Key ethical questions involve the potential for AI to perpetuate existing inequalities, privacy breaches, and the delegation of critical decisions to machines. For instance, biased algorithms can reinforce discrimination in areas such as hiring and lending, exacerbating social disparities. Privacy concerns arise from the extensive data collection and surveillance capabilities of AI, potentially infringing on individuals' rights to privacy and autonomy. Philosophical approaches such as utilitarianism evaluate AI's consequences based on overall happiness or harm, while deontological frameworks focus on duties and rights regardless of outcomes, ensuring that ethical principles are upheld even if the results are not universally beneficial.

Practically, embedding ethical considerations into AI development involves implementing guidelines that ensure respect for human rights, dignity, and privacy. This can include conducting regular audits to identify and mitigate bias in AI systems, as well as ensuring data protection through robust encryption and anonymization techniques. Organizations like the IEEE have developed standards and recommendations to guide ethical AI development, emphasizing transparency, accountability, and harm prevention. These standards encourage developers to create AI systems that are explainable and interpretable, enabling users to understand how decisions are made and to challenge them if necessary. By adhering to these ethical guidelines, the AI community can work toward building systems that are not only technologically advanced but also socially responsible and equitable.

BIAS IN AI ALGORITHMS

Bias in AI systems can stem from various sources, including skewed data sets, the subjective nature of algorithm design, and the unconscious biases of developers. These biases can manifest in several detrimental ways, such as racial bias in facial recognition technologies and gender bias in job recommendation algorithms. To combat these issues, AI developers can employ techniques like diversifying training data, applying algorithmic fairness interventions, and conducting rigorous bias audits. Notable instances, like the biased performance of facial recognition across different demographics, have highlighted the need for more robust measures to address bias in AI technologies. Additionally, ongoing research into algorithmic fairness and interpretability aims to develop frameworks that mitigate bias while ensuring transparency and accountability in AI decision-making processes. Through initiative-taking measures and interdisciplinary collaboration, the AI community can work toward building more equitable and trustworthy AI systems that benefit society.

FAIRNESS AND ACCOUNTABILITY

Fairness in AI involves creating systems that are equitable and do not unduly discriminate against any individual or group. This can be approached by designing algorithms that ensure equal opportunity, treatment, and impact across diverse groups. Accountability in AI refers to the mechanisms by which organizations ensure their AI systems adhere to ethical and legal standards, such as implementing audit trails, enhancing model explainability, and maintaining operational transparency. Examples include the use of impact assessments and the development of tools like IBM's Fairness 360 Kit, which helps developers detect and mitigate bias in machine learning models. Additionally, regulatory frameworks like the General Data Protection Regulation (GDPR) in Europe and the Algorithmic Accountability Act in the

United States aim to hold organizations accountable for the ethical use of AI technologies, fostering a culture of responsible AI development and deployment.

REGULATION AND GOVERNANCE

The regulation of AI varies significantly across different geographic regions. The European Union's General Data Protection Regulation (GDPR) includes provisions that affect how AI manages personal data, emphasizing user consent, data minimization, and the right to explanation. In contrast, the United States adopts a more sector-specific approach, focusing on areas like healthcare and transportation without overarching AI legislation. Looking forward, there is growing advocacy for international standards and frameworks that can guide the global development and deployment of AI technologies, suggesting a future where AI governance is more unified and standardized. Initiatives such as the Global Partnership on Artificial Intelligence (GPAI) aim to facilitate collaboration among nations to address familiar challenges and establish ethical guidelines for AI development and deployment on a global scale. This collaborative approach seeks to balance innovation with ethical considerations and ensure that AI benefits society.

AI APPLICATION: ANALYZE BIAS IN A DATASET AND DISCUSS MITIGATION STRATEGIES

In this AI Application, users will analyze bias in a dataset and discuss mitigation strategies using Python, Pandas, and Fairlearn. This guide provides step-by-step instructions to identify and mitigate biases using fairness metrics, including:

- *Step 1*: Set Up Development Environment
- *Step 2*: Load the Dataset
- *Step 3*: Preprocess the Data
- *Step 4*: Train a Baseline Model
- *Step 5*: Analyze Bias in the Model
- *Step 6*: Run the Script

Step 1: Set Up Development Environment

1. Install Python

   a. Follow the instructions in the previous examples to download and install Python.

2. Install Necessary Libraries

   a. Open a terminal or command prompt.
   b. Install the required libraries by typing:
   pip install pandas scikit-learn fairlearn

Step 2: Load and Explore the Dataset

1. Open Code Editor

   a. Use preferred text editor or IDE.

2. Create a New Python File

   a. Create a new file named "bias_analysis.py."

3. Import Necessary Libraries

   a. At the top of the "bias_analysis.py" file, import the necessary libraries:

```
1   import pandas as pd
2   import matplotlib.pyplot as plt
3   from sklearn.model_selection import train_test_split
4   from sklearn.linear_model import LogisticRegression
5   from sklearn.metrics import accuracy_score, confusion_matrix, classification_report
6   from imblearn.over_sampling import SMOTE
7   import warnings
```

4. Load the Dataset

   a. For this example, use the UCI Adult dataset, which is known to have biases. Download it from the UCI Machine Learning Repository or use a local copy.
   b. Load the dataset into a Pandas DataFrame.

```
11    # Load and preprocess the dataset
12    df = pd.read_csv('adult.csv')
13    df = df.dropna()
```

Step 3: Preprocess the Data

1. Preprocess the Data

   a. Manage missing values, encode categorical variables, and split the data into training and testing sets:

```
15   # Convert 'income' column to binary (0 and 1) based on '>50K' and '<=50K'
16   df['income'] = df['income'].apply(lambda x: 1 if x.strip() == '>50K' else 0)
17
```

```
26   # Split the data into training and testing sets using stratification
27   X_train, X_test, Y_train, Y_test = train_test_split(X, Y, test_size=0.2, stratify=Y, random_state=42)
```

Step 4: Train a Baseline Model

1. Train the Model

   a. Train a logistic regression model on the training data.

```
43   # Train the logistic regression model
44   model = LogisticRegression(max_iter=1000)
45   model.fit(X_train, Y_train)
```

2. Evaluate the Model

   a. Evaluate the model on the test data.

```
47   # Predict and evaluate the model
48   Y_pred = model.predict(X_test)
49   print("Accuracy:", accuracy_score(Y_test, Y_pred))
50   print("Confusion Matrix:\n", confusion_matrix(Y_test, Y_pred))
51   print("Classification Report:\n", classification_report(Y_test, Y_pred))
```

Step 5: Analyze Bias in the Model

1. Analyze Bias

   a. Identify the sensitive attribute (e.g., "gender" or "race") and analyze the model's performance across distinct groups.

```
31   # Analyze bias
32   sensitive_feature = X_test['gender_Male']
33   metric_frame = MetricFrame(metrics=accuracy_score, y_true=Y_test, y_pred=Y_pred, sensitive_features=sensitive_feature)
34   print("Overall Accuracy:", metric_frame.overall)
35   print("Accuracy by Group:\n", metric_frame.by_group)
36
37   demographic_parity_diff = demographic_parity_difference(y_true=Y_test, y_pred=Y_pred, sensitive_features=sensitive_feature)
38   print("Demographic Parity Difference:", demographic_parity_diff)
```

2. Fairness Metrics

    a. Calculate fairness metrics such as demographic parity difference.

```
37  demographic_parity_diff = demographic_parity_difference(y_true=Y_test, y_pred=Y_pred, sensitive_features=sensitive_feature)
38  print("Demographic Parity Difference:", demographic_parity_diff)
```

Step 6: Mitigate Bias

1. Mitigate Bias

    a. Use Fairlearn's reduction algorithms to mitigate bias. For example, user's can use the GridSearch algorithm with a demographic parity constraint.

```
# Mitigate bias
constraint = DemographicParity()
mitigator = GridSearch(estimator=LogisticRegression(max_iter=1000), constraints=constraint)
mitigator.fit(X_train, Y_train, sensitive_features=X_train['gender_Male'])

# Get the best mitigated model (using fairlearn's selection criteria, not a direct attribute like best_estimator_)
best_index = np.argmax([demographic_parity_difference(y_true=Y_train, y_pred=model.predict(X_train), sensitive_features=X_train['gender_Male']) for model
mitigated_model = mitigator.predictors_[best_index]
```

2. Evaluate the Mitigated Model

    a. Evaluate the mitigated model on the test data.

```
49  # Evaluate the mitigated model
50  Y_pred_mitigated = mitigated_model.predict(X_test)
51  print("Mitigated Model Accuracy:", accuracy_score(Y_test, Y_pred_mitigated))
52  print("Mitigated Model Classification Report:\n", classification_report(Y_test, Y_pred_mitigated))
53  demographic_parity_diff_mitigated = demographic_parity_difference(y_true=Y_test, y_pred=Y_pred_mitigated, sensitive_features=sensitive_feature)
54  print("Mitigated Model Demographic Parity Difference:", demographic_parity_diff_mitigated)
```

3. Complete Script

    a. The complete "bias_analysis.py" file should look like this.

```
1   import pandas as pd
2   import numpy as np
3   from sklearn.model_selection import train_test_split
4   from sklearn.linear_model import LogisticRegression
5   from sklearn.metrics import accuracy_score, confusion_matrix, classification_report
6   from fairlearn.metrics import MetricFrame, demographic_parity_difference
7   from fairlearn.reductions import GridSearch, DemographicParity
8   import matplotlib.pyplot as plt
9
10  # Load the dataset
11  df = pd.read_csv('adult.csv')
12  print(df.head())
13
14  # Preprocess the data
15  df = df.dropna()
16  df = pd.get_dummies(df)
17  X = df.drop('income_>50K', axis=1)
18  Y = df['income_>50K']
19  X_train, X_test, Y_train, Y_test = train_test_split(X, Y, test_size=0.2, random_state=42)
20
```

```
21   # Train the model
22   model = LogisticRegression(max_iter=1000)
23   model.fit(X_train, Y_train)
24
25   # Evaluate the model
26   Y_pred = model.predict(X_test)
27   print("Accuracy:", accuracy_score(Y_test, Y_pred))
28   print("Confusion Matrix:\n", confusion_matrix(Y_test, Y_pred))
29   print("Classification Report:\n", classification_report(Y_test, Y_pred))
30
31   # Analyze bias
32   sensitive_feature = X_test['gender_Male']
33   metric_frame = MetricFrame(metrics=accuracy_score, y_true=Y_test, y_pred=Y_pred, sensitive_features=sensitive_feature)
34   print("Overall Accuracy:", metric_frame.overall)
35   print("Accuracy by Group:\n", metric_frame.by_group)
36
37   demographic_parity_diff = demographic_parity_difference(y_true=Y_test, y_pred=Y_pred, sensitive_features=sensitive_feature)
38   print("Demographic Parity Difference:", demographic_parity_diff)
39
```

```
40   # Mitigate bias
41   constraint = DemographicParity()
42   mitigator = GridSearch(estimator=LogisticRegression(max_iter=1000), constraints=constraint)
43   mitigator.fit(X_train, Y_train, sensitive_features=X_train['gender_Male'])
44
45   # Get the best mitigated model (using Fairlearn's selection criteria, not a direct attribute like best_estimator_)
46   best_index = np.argmax([demographic_parity_difference(y_true=Y_train, y_pred=model.predict(X_train), sensitive_features=X_train['gender_Male']) for mode
47   mitigated_model = mitigator.predictors_[best_index]
48
49   # Evaluate the mitigated model
50   Y_pred_mitigated = mitigated_model.predict(X_test)
51   print("Mitigated Model Accuracy:", accuracy_score(Y_test, Y_pred_mitigated))
52   print("Mitigated Model Classification Report:\n", classification_report(Y_test, Y_pred_mitigated))
53   demographic_parity_diff_mitigated = demographic_parity_difference(y_true=Y_test, y_pred=Y_pred_mitigated, sensitive_features=sensitive_feature)
54   print("Mitigated Model Demographic Parity Difference:", demographic_parity_diff_mitigated)
```

Step 7: Run the Script

1. Run the Script

   a. Open a terminal or command prompt.

   b. Navigate to the directory where the "bias_analysis.py" file is located.

   c. Run the script by typing:
      python bias_analysis.py

2. View the Results:

   a. The script will print the accuracy, confusion matrix, classification report, and fairness metrics for both the baseline and mitigated models to the console.

```
PS C:\Users\erik\Downloads\OneDrive-2024-06-06> & c:/Users/erik/Downloads/OneDrive-2024-06-06/PIL/Scripts/python.exe c:/Users/erik/Downloads/OneDrive-2024-06-06/bias_analysis.py
   age     workclass  fnlwgt   education  education_num   marital_status      occupation  ...   race  gender capital_gain  capital_loss  hours_per_week  native_country  income
0   39     State-gov   77516   Bachelors           13       Never-married    Adm-clerical  ...  White    Male         2174             0              40   United-States   <=50K
1   50  Self-emp-not-inc 83311  Bachelors          13  Married-civ-spouse  Exec-managerial  ...  White    Male            0             0              13   United-States   <=50K
2   38       Private  215646     HS-grad            9            Divorced  Handlers-cleaners ...  White    Male            0             0              40   United-States   <=50K
3   53       Private  234721        11th            7  Married-civ-spouse  Handlers-cleaners ...  Black    Male            0             0              40   United-States   <=50K
4   28       Private  338409   Bachelors           13  Married-civ-spouse     Prof-specialty ...  Black  Female            0             0              40            Cuba   <=50K

[5 rows x 15 columns]
C:\Users\erik\Downloads\OneDrive-2024-06-06\PIL\Lib\site-packages\sklearn\linear_model\_logistic.py:469: ConvergenceWarning: lbfgs failed to converge (status=1):
STOP: TOTAL NO. of ITERATIONS REACHED LIMIT.

Increase the number of iterations (max_iter) or scale the data as shown in:
    https://scikit-learn.org/stable/modules/preprocessing.html
Please also refer to the documentation for alternative solver options:
    https://scikit-learn.org/stable/modules/linear_model.html#logistic-regression
  n_iter_i = _check_optimize_result(
Accuracy: 0.5
Confusion Matrix:
 [[2 0]
 [2 0]]
C:\Users\erik\Downloads\OneDrive-2024-06-06\PIL\Lib\site-packages\sklearn\metrics\_classification.py:1517: UndefinedMetricWarning: Precision is ill-defined and being set to 0.0 in labels wit
h no predicted samples. Use `zero_division` parameter to control this behavior.
  _warn_prf(average, modifier, f"{metric.capitalize()} is", len(result))
C:\Users\erik\Downloads\OneDrive-2024-06-06\PIL\Lib\site-packages\sklearn\metrics\_classification.py:1517: UndefinedMetricWarning: Precision is ill-defined and being set to 0.0 in labels wit
h no predicted samples. Use `zero_division` parameter to control this behavior.
  _warn_prf(average, modifier, f"{metric.capitalize()} is", len(result))
C:\Users\erik\Downloads\OneDrive-2024-06-06\PIL\Lib\site-packages\sklearn\metrics\_classification.py:1517: UndefinedMetricWarning: Precision is ill-defined and being set to 0.0 in labels wit
h no predicted samples. Use `zero_division` parameter to control this behavior.
  _warn_prf(average, modifier, f"{metric.capitalize()} is", len(result))
```

```
Classification Report:
              precision    recall  f1-score   support

       False       0.50      1.00      0.67         2
        True       0.00      0.00      0.00         2

    accuracy                           0.50         4
   macro avg       0.25      0.50      0.33         4
weighted avg       0.25      0.50      0.33         4

Overall Accuracy: 0.5
Accuracy by Group:
 gender Male
False    0.666667
True     0.000000
Name: accuracy_score, dtype: float64
Demographic Parity Difference: 0.0
C:\Users\erik\Downloads\OneDrive-2024-06-06\PIL\Lib\site-packages\fairlearn\reductions\_moments\utility_parity.py:214: FutureWarning: ChainedAssignmentError: behaviour will change in pandas
3.0!
You are setting values through chained assignment. Currently this works in certain cases, but when using Copy-on-Write (which will become the default behaviour in pandas 3.0) this will never
work to update the original DataFrame or Series, because the intermediate object on which we are setting values will behave as a copy.
A typical example is when you are setting values in a column of a DataFrame, like:

df["col"][row_indexer] = value

Use `df.loc[row_indexer, "col"] = values` instead, to perform the assignment in a single step and ensure this keeps updating the original `df`.

See the caveats in the documentation: https://pandas.pydata.org/pandas-docs/stable/user_guide/indexing.html#returning-a-view-versus-a-copy
```

Following these steps enables users to successfully analyze bias in a dataset and discuss mitigation strategies using Python, Pandas, and Fairlearn. This exercise demonstrates how to identify and mitigate biases in machine learning models, providing a practical understanding of ethical considerations in AI.

CONCLUSION

This chapter calls for a concerted effort among all stakeholders in AI—developers, regulators, and the public—to address ethical challenges proactively. It is crucial for the future of AI that these issues are not only recognized but actively countered through informed policymaking, responsible development practices, and continuous public engagement. The goal is to ensure AI technologies advance societal well-being, enhance fairness, and remain under meaningful human control.

This comprehensive approach in the chapter provides a solid foundation for understanding the ethical, bias-related, fairness, and regulatory issues in AI, empowering readers to contribute positively to the discourse on responsible AI development and implementation.

## CHAPTER 7

AI IN PRACTICE: INDUSTRY CASE STUDIES

U nderstanding AI's theoretical aspects is best achieved through examining its practical applications. This chapter presents a series of illuminating case studies from key industries such as healthcare, finance, transportation, retail, and manufacturing, highlighting how AI technologies are being effectively implemented to address real-world challenges. These case studies not only underscore the versatility and potency of AI but also shed light on the industry-specific obstacles and triumphs encountered in the adoption of AI solutions. By delving into concrete examples across diverse sectors, this chapter offers valuable insights into the current landscape of AI deployment and its transformative impact on various industries.

HEALTHCARE

AI is transforming healthcare with innovations such as machine learning models that predict patient health outcomes and AI-driven diagnostics that enhance imaging and pathology analyses. Tools like IBM Watson are instrumental in personalized medicine, analyzing patient data against a vast array of previously resolved cases. Discuss the use of AI in early cancer detection, highlighting how it enhances the accuracy of screening mammograms and reduces false positives and negatives, with findings supported by studies in journals like *JAMA Oncology*. Evaluate the role of AI in reducing operational costs, improving patient care efficiency, and addressing ethical concerns related to patient data privacy and the potential for biased algorithms in treatment recommendations.

FINANCE

AI in finance automates complex tasks such as risk management, investment predictions, and fraud detection. Systems like KAI, developed for banking applications, use NLP to interact with users, providing financial advice and customer support. They also detail the use of AI in detecting credit card fraud, where real-time algorithms analyze transaction patterns and flag anomalies, significantly lowering fraud rates for companies like Visa and Mastercard. Further, they discuss how AI-driven automation in trading and customer service not only reduces operational costs and enhances decision-making but also raises concerns about job displacement and the necessity for transparent AI systems.

TRANSPORTATION

AI is revolutionizing healthcare by introducing innovations like machine learning models that forecast patient health trajectories and AI-powered diagnostics that refine imaging and pathology assessments. Solutions like IBM Watson are pivotal in personalized medicine, scrutinizing patient data against extensive databases of resolved cases. Explore AI's role in early cancer detection, emphasizing its enhancement of screening mammogram accuracy and reduction of false positives and negatives, substantiated by studies in prestigious journals like *JAMA Oncology*. Assess AI's impact on curtailing operational expenses, enhancing patient care efficacy, and mitigating ethical dilemmas concerning patient data confidentiality and the risk of biased algorithms in treatment suggestions. These advancements not only streamline healthcare delivery but also pave the way for more precise and patient-centric medical interventions.

RETAIL

AI revolutionizes retail by personalizing shopping experiences through recommendation algorithms and optimizing inventory management with predictive analytics. Tools like Amazon's recommendation engine utilize customer data to suggest products, thereby enhancing user experiences and boosting sales. Look at how AI is employed in customer service chatbots in retail, focusing on companies like Sephora and H&M, which use these bots to manage inquiries and provide shopping advice, leading to improved customer satisfaction and reduced operational costs. Analyze the increase in efficiency and customer engagement that AI brings to retail, while also addressing challenges related to data privacy and the potential for creating consumer profiles without consent.

MANUFACTURING

AI applications in manufacturing transform the sector by enabling predictive maintenance, enhancing quality control through machine vision, and optimizing supply chains with AI-driven logistics planning. Focus on the role of AI in predictive maintenance within heavy industries, exemplified by GE's use of AI to forecast equipment failures before they happen, thereby minimizing downtime and extending machinery life. Evaluate how AI boosts production rates and product quality, reduces waste, and consider the challenges manufacturers encounter, such as the substantial initial investment required for AI technology and the ongoing need for worker retraining.

AI APPLICATION: PREDICTING PATIENT OUTCOMES IN HEALTHCARE

In this AI application, users will create a case study for predicting patient outcomes in healthcare using Python and Scikit-learn. This guide provides step-by-step instructions to build a predictive model, including data preprocessing, feature engineering, model training, and evaluation, including:

- *Step 1*: Set Up Development Environment

- *Step 2*: Load and Explore the Healthcare Dataset

- *Step 3*: Preprocess the Data

- *Step 4*: Train a Predictive Model

- *Step 5*: Evaluate the Model

- *Step 6*: Run the Script

Step 1: Set Up Development Environment

1. Install Python:

   • Follow the instructions in the previous examples to download and install Python.

2. Install Necessary Libraries:

   • Open a terminal or command prompt.

   • Install the required libraries by typing:

   pip install pandas scikit-learn

Step 2: Load and Explore the Healthcare Dataset

1. Open Code Editor:

   • Use preferred text editor or IDE.

2. Create a New Python File:

   • Create a new file named "healthcare_prediction.py."

3. Import Necessary Libraries:

   At the top of the "healthcare_prediction.py" file, import the necessary libraries:

```
1   import pandas as pd
2   from sklearn.model_selection import train_test_split
3   from sklearn.preprocessing import StandardScaler
4   from sklearn.linear_model import LogisticRegression
5   from sklearn.metrics import accuracy_score, confusion_matrix, classification_report
```

4. Load the Dataset:

   • For this example, use a sample healthcare dataset. Download it from a public repository or use a local copy. Here, assume the dataset is named "healthcare_data.csv."

   • Load the dataset into a Pandas DataFrame:

```
7    # Load the dataset
8    try:
9        df = pd.read_csv('healthcare_data.csv')
10       print(df.head())
11   except FileNotFoundError:
```

5. Explore the Dataset:

- Print the first few rows of the dataset to understand its structure:

```
7    # Load the dataset
8    try:
9        df = pd.read_csv('healthcare_data.csv')
10       print(df.head())
11   except FileNotFoundError:
```

Step 3: Preprocess the Data

1. Handle Missing Values:

- Identify and manage missing values:

```
20    # Preprocess the data
21    df = df.dropna()
```

2. Encode Categorical Variables:

- Convert categorical variables to numeric using one-hot encoding:

```
31    # Convert categorical variables to dummy variables
32    df = pd.get_dummies(df)
```

3. Split the Data into Features and Target Variable:

- Define input features (X) and target variable (Y):

```
34    # Split the DataFrame into features and target variable
35    X = df.drop('outcome', axis=1)
36    Y = df['outcome']
```

4. Split the Data into Training and Testing Sets:

- Split the data into training and testing sets:

```
38    # Splitting the dataset into the Training set and Test set
39    X_train, X_test, Y_train, Y_test = train_test_split(X, Y, test_size=0.2, random_state=42)
```

5. Standardize the Data:

- Standardize the data to have zero mean and unit variance:

```
41    # Feature Scaling
42    scaler = StandardScaler()
43    X_train = scaler.fit_transform(X_train)
44    X_test = scaler.transform(X_test)
```

Step 4: Train a Predictive Model

1. Train the Model:

- Train a logistic regression model on the training data:

```
46    # Train the model
47    model = LogisticRegression(max_iter=1000)
48    try:
49        model.fit(X_train, Y_train)
50    except Exception as e:
51        print(f"Error during model training: {e}")
52        exit()
```

Step 5: Evaluate the Model

1. Make Predictions:

- Make predictions on the test data:

```
54    # Make predictions
55    Y_pred = model.predict(X_test)
```

2. Evaluate the Model:

- Calculate and print the accuracy score, confusion matrix, and classification report:

```
57    # Evaluate the model
58    accuracy = accuracy_score(Y_test, Y_pred)
59    print("Accuracy:", accuracy)
60    print("Confusion Matrix:\n", confusion_matrix(Y_test, Y_pred))
61    print("Classification are available only in the next cell after you run it.Report:\n", classification_report(Y_test, Y_pred))
```

3. Complete Script:

- The complete "healthcare_prediction.py" file should look like this:

```
AI_Revealed > ⌖ ai_revealed_chp_7_code_healthcare_predictions.py > ...
 1    import pandas as pd
 2    from sklearn.model_selection import train_test_split
 3    from sklearn.preprocessing import StandardScaler
 4    from sklearn.linear_model import LogisticRegression
 5    from sklearn.metrics import accuracy_score, confusion_matrix, classification_report
 6
 7    # Load the dataset
 8    try:
 9        df = pd.read_csv('healthcare_data.csv')
10        print(df.head())
11    except FileNotFoundError:
12        print("Error: The file 'healthcare_data.csv' does not exist. Please check the file path.")
13        exit()
14
15    # Check for 'outcome' column in the dataset
16    if 'outcome' not in df.columns:
17        print("Error: The dataset must include an 'outcome' column.")
18        exit()
19
20    # Preprocess the data
21    df = df.dropna()
22    if df.empty:
23        print("Error: No data remains after dropping rows with missing values.")
24        exit()
25
26    # Ensure that the dataset has more than one category in 'outcome'
27    if df['outcome'].nunique() < 2:
28        print("Error: The target variable 'outcome' must have at least two categories.")
29        exit()
30
31    # Convert categorical variables to dummy variables
32    df = pd.get_dummies(df)
33
34    # Split the Dataframe into features and target variable
35    X = df.drop('outcome', axis=1)
36    Y = df['outcome']
37
38    # Splitting the dataset into the Training set and Test set
39    X_train, X_test, Y_train, Y_test = train_test_split(X, Y, test_size=0.2, random_state=42)
40
41    # Feature Scaling
42    scaler = StandardScaler()
43    X_train = scaler.fit_transform(X_train)
44    X_test = scaler.transform(X_test)
45
46    # Train the model
47    model = LogisticRegression(max_iter=1000)
48    try:
49        model.fit(X_train, Y_train)
50    except Exception as e:
51        print(f"Error during model training: {e}")
52        exit()
53
54    # Make predictions
55    Y_pred = model.predict(X_test)
56
57    # Evaluate the model
58    accuracy = accuracy_score(Y_test, Y_pred)
59    print("Accuracy:", accuracy)
60    print("Confusion Matrix:\n", confusion_matrix(Y_test, Y_pred))
61    print("Classification are available only in the next cell after you run it.Report:\n", classification_report(Y_test, Y_pred))
```

CONCLUSION

This module has showcased the diverse and transformative applications of AI across several key industries, including healthcare, finance, transportation, retail, and manufacturing. Through detailed case studies, readers have seen how AI technologies are addressing real-world challenges, driving innovation, and enhancing efficiency in these sectors. The versatility and effectiveness of AI are evident, but so are the unique obstacles and triumphs each industry faces in its AI journey.

By examining these concrete examples, readers gain a deeper understanding of the current landscape of AI deployment. These insights not only highlight the potential of AI to revolutionize various fields but also emphasize the importance of strategic implementation and continuous adaptation to industry-specific needs. As AI continues to evolve, its impact will undoubtedly expand, offering even greater opportunities for innovation and improvement in countless areas of our lives.

## CHAPTER 8

FUTURE OF AI AND EMERGING TECHNOLOGIES

In this chapter, the focus is on the continual evolution of artificial intelligence (AI) and the emergence of innovative technologies that promise to reshape the AI landscape. This chapter investigates innovative developments such as quantum computing, edge AI, and explainable AI, discussing their potential to revolutionize how AI systems interact with their environment.

Quantum computing represents a change in basic assumptions in computational power, offering the potential to solve complex problems at an unprecedented scale and speed. This technology holds promise for enhancing AI capabilities by tackling challenges that are currently beyond the reach of classical computing methods.

Additionally, the chapter explores the concept of edge AI, which enables AI algorithms to run directly on devices, reducing latency and enhancing privacy by processing data locally. This approach is particularly relevant for applications requiring real-time decision-making, such as autonomous vehicles and smart IoT devices.

Ethical considerations play a crucial role in shaping the future of AI and its applications. As AI becomes more ubiquitous, it is essential to address issues related to fairness, accountability, and transparency. By fostering discussions on these topics, the chapter encourages readers to think critically about the ethical implications of AI technologies and their impact on society.

Overall, Chapter 8 serves as a thought-provoking exploration of the future trajectory of AI, highlighting both the transformative potential of emerging technologies and the ethical challenges that must be addressed to ensure their responsible deployment.

QUANTUM COMPUTING

Quantum computing holds the promise of revolutionizing AI by providing unprecedented computational power that can execute complex algorithms exponentially faster than traditional computers. This groundbreaking technology harnesses the principles of quantum mechanics to process information in fundamentally diverse ways, enabling the manipulation of complex variables and the execution of simultaneous computations.

The potential applications of quantum computing in AI are vast, and they possess the capacity to significantly enhance capabilities in fields such as drug discovery. Quantum computers could analyze molecular structures with unprecedented detail and at a fraction of the time required by current computational methods. As industry leaders like Google and IBM make strides in developing more stable quantum computing systems, the prospect of breakthroughs that could dramatically shorten AI model training times and enhance predictive accuracy becomes increasingly feasible.

Moreover, quantum computing has the potential to revolutionize cryptography and optimization problems, further expanding the scope of its impact on AI and other fields. While challenges such as maintaining quantum coherence and error correction persist, ongoing research and development efforts hold the promise of unlocking the full potential of quantum computing and reshaping the future of AI as we know it.

EDGE AI

Edge AI, short for edge artificial intelligence, marks a change in basic assumptions in AI deployment, moving computation from centralized cloud servers to local devices. By processing data on the device itself, edge AI significantly reduces latency, ensuring rapid responses critical for real-time applications like autonomous vehicles and healthcare monitoring. Moreover, this approach conserves bandwidth by minimizing the need for data transmission to remote servers, a boon for bandwidth-constrained environments or scenarios with unreliable network connectivity.

Privacy is another paramount benefit of edge AI. By keeping data local, sensitive information remains on the device, reducing the risk of unauthorized access or data breaches. This is particularly vital in sectors like healthcare, where patient confidentiality is sacrosanct.

Advancements in microprocessor technology have fueled the proliferation of edge AI, enabling powerful computational capabilities in compact, energy-efficient devices. Consumer products like smartphones and smart home devices now leverage edge AI to deliver faster, more responsive user experiences.

As edge AI continues to mature, its impact extends beyond consumer electronics into industrial automation, smart cities, and beyond. With its ability to process data closer to the source, edge AI promises to unlock new levels of efficiency, autonomy, and intelligence across various domains, heralding a future where AI is seamlessly integrated into the fabric of everyday lives.

EXPLAINABLE AI

Explainable AI (XAI) is a critical response to the growing complexity and opacity of modern AI systems. In sectors like healthcare, finance, and law, where AI-driven decisions can have profound real-world consequences, the need for transparency and accountability is paramount. XAI seeks to demystify the inner workings of AI models, making their outputs interpretable and understandable to humans.

By providing insights into how AI arrives at its decisions, XAI enhances trust and confidence in AI systems, enabling stakeholders to validate and verify the reasoning behind AI-driven outcomes. This transparency is not only crucial for ensuring fairness and accountability but also for identifying and mitigating biases that may be present in the data or algorithms.

Regulatory frameworks, such as the EU's General Data Protection Regulation (GDPR), underscore the importance of explainability in AI systems. The GDPR's right to explanation empowers individuals to demand transparency about the logic behind automated decisions that affect them, reinforcing the need for AI systems to be interpretable and accountable.

As AI continues to permeate diverse aspects of society, the adoption of XAI principles becomes increasingly imperative. By promoting transparency, interpretability, and accountability, XAI paves the way for the responsible and ethical deployment of AI technologies in the modern world.

AI FOR SOCIAL GOOD

AI's potential for social good is increasingly recognized as it transcends conventional boundaries to tackle global challenges. Microsoft's AI for Earth initiative exemplifies this by leveraging AI to monitor environmental changes, optimize agriculture, and forecast climate shifts, demonstrating how technology can contribute to sustainable development.

In public health, AI plays a pivotal role in pandemic response, enabling rapid diagnosis, contact tracing, and resource allocation. Moreover, AI-driven disaster management systems utilize data from drones and satellites to coordinate efficient relief efforts, minimizing human suffering and enhancing disaster resilience.

These endeavors underscore AI's capacity to address complex societal issues, emphasizing the importance of ethical considerations and human-centric approaches. By aligning AI initiatives with ethical guidelines and prioritizing inclusivity, transparency, and accountability, technology can empower communities, amplify their voices, and promote equity and social justice.

As AI continues to evolve, its impact on social good is poised to expand further. By fostering collaboration between technologists, policymakers, and communities, we can harness AI's potential to drive positive change, foster sustainable development, and create a more equitable and resilient future for all.

AI APPLICATION: EXPERIMENT WITH A SIMPLE QUANTUM COMPUTING ALGORITHM USING IBM'S QISKIT

In this AI application, readers will experiment with a simple quantum computing algorithm using IBM's Qiskit. This guide introduces quantum computing basics and step-by-step instructions for implementing a basic quantum algorithm, including:

- *Step 1*: Set Up Development Environment

- *Step 2*: Introduction to Quantum Computing Basics

- *Step 3*: Introduction to Quantum Computing Basics

- *Step 4*: Run the Script

Step 1: Set Up Development Environment

1. Install Python:

    - Follow the instructions in the previous examples to download and install Python.

2. Install Qiskit:

    - Open a terminal or command prompt.

    - Install Qiskit by typing:

      pip install qiskit

Step 2: Introduction to Quantum Computing Basics

Quantum computing leverages the principles of quantum mechanics to process information in fundamentally separate ways compared to classical computing. Following are some of the key concepts.

- *Qubits*: Quantum bits, or qubits, are the basic units of quantum information. Unlike classical bits, which can be 0 or 1, qubits can exist in superpositions of states.

- *Superposition*: A qubit can be in a state of 0, 1, or any superposition of these states.

- *Entanglement*: Qubits can be entangled, meaning the state of one qubit can depend on the state of another, no matter the distance between them.

- *Quantum Gates*: Operations that change the state of qubits, like logic gates in classical computing.

Step 3: Implement a Basic Quantum Algorithm

1. Open the Code Editor:

    • Use preferred text editor or IDE.

2. Create a New Python File:

    • Create a new file named "ai_revealed_chp_8_code_quantum_algorithm.py."

3. Import Necessary Libraries:

    • At the top of the "quantum_algorithm.py" file, import the necessary libraries:

```
8    # Create a Quantum Circuit with 2 qubits and 2 classical bits
9    qc = QuantumCircuit(2, 2)
10
11   # Apply Hadamard gate to the first qubit to create superposition
12   qc.h(0)
13
14   # Apply CNOT gate with the first qubit as control and the second qubit as targe
15   qc.cx(0, 1)
16
17   # Measure the qubits
18   qc.measure([0, 1], [0, 1])
19
20   # Draw the circuit
21   output_file.write(str(qc.draw()) + "\n")
```

4. Create a Quantum Circuit:

    • Create a quantum circuit with two qubits and two classical bits:

```
1    output_file = open('ai_revealed_chp_8_code_quantum_algorithm_output.txt', 'w')
2    import qiskit
3    from qiskit import QuantumCircuit, transpile
4    from qiskit_aer import Aer
5    from qiskit.visualization import plot_histogram
6    import matplotlib.pyplot as plt
```

5. Simulate the Quantum Circuit:

- Use the Aer simulator to simulate the quantum circuit:

```
23    # Use Aer's qasm_simulator
24    simulator = Aer.get_backend('qasm_simulator')
25
26    # Transpile the circuit for the simulator
27    transpiled_circuit = transpile(qc, simulator)
28
29    # Run the transpiled circuit on the simulator
30    job = simulator.run(transpiled_circuit, shots=1000)
31
32    # Grab results from the job
33    result = job.result()
34
35    # Returns counts
36    counts = result.get_counts(qc)
37    output_file.write(str("\nTotal count for 00 and 11 are:", counts) + "\n")
38
39    # Plot a histogram
40    plot_histogram(counts)
41    plt.show()
42    output_file.close()
```

6. Complete Script:

- The complete "quantum_algorithm.py" file should look like this:

```
1     output_file = open('ai_revealed_chp_8_code_quantum_algorithm_output.txt', 'w')
2     import qiskit
3     from qiskit import QuantumCircuit, transpile
4     from qiskit_aer import Aer
5     from qiskit.visualization import plot_histogram
6     import matplotlib.pyplot as plt
7
8     # Create a Quantum Circuit with 2 qubits and 2 classical bits
9     qc = QuantumCircuit(2, 2)
10
11    # Apply Hadamard gate to the first qubit to create superposition
12    qc.h(0)
13
14    # Apply CNOT gate with the first qubit as control and the second qubit as target
15    qc.cx(0, 1)
16
17    # Measure the qubits
18    qc.measure([0, 1], [0, 1])
19
20    # Draw the circuit
21    output_file.write(str(qc.draw()) + "\n")
22
23    # Use Aer's qasm_simulator
24    simulator = Aer.get_backend('qasm_simulator')
25
26    # Transpile the circuit for the simulator
27    transpiled_circuit = transpile(qc, simulator)
28
29    # Run the transpiled circuit on the simulator
30    job = simulator.run(transpiled_circuit, shots=1000)
31
32    # Grab results from the job
33    result = job.result()
34
35    # Returns counts
36    counts = result.get_counts(qc)
37    output_file.write(str("\nTotal count for 00 and 11 are:", counts) + "\n")
38
39    # Plot a histogram
40    plot_histogram(counts)
41    plt.show()
42    output_file.close()
```

7. Run the Script:

Python algorithm.py.

```
Python files >  ☰ ai_revealed_chp_8_code_quantum_algorithm_output.txt
1
2    q_0: ┤ H ├──■──┤M├────────
3
4    q_1: ──────┤ X ├──┤M├
5
6    c: 2/═══════════════════
7                    0  1
```

CONCLUSION

This chapter offers a comprehensive look at the emerging technologies shaping the future of AI. By digging into how these advancements integrate into everyday lives and global challenges, it encourages a broader understanding and critical reflection on the path AI is set to take in reshaping the world.

## CHAPTER 9

GETTING STARTED WITH AI DEVELOPMENT

This chapter serves as a comprehensive guide for individuals venturing into AI development. It offers practical insights on establishing a development environment, advocating Python as a versatile programming language ideal for AI endeavors. With a focus on imparting foundational skills and fostering best practices, this chapter empowers aspiring AI developers to embark on their journey with confidence, armed with the requisite tools and expertise to initiate and navigate their own AI projects effectively. Whether understanding neural networks or exploring machine learning (ML) algorithms, this resource equips enthusiasts with the essential knowledge and resources to forge ahead in the dynamic realm of AI development.

SETTING UP DEVELOPMENT ENVIRONMENT

Setting up a conducive development environment lays the foundation for successful AI endeavors. It entails meticulous selection of both hardware and software components capable of managing the computational demands and voluminous datasets inherent to AI tasks. Primarily, developers should commence by installing Python, recognized as the de facto programming language in the AI domain owing to its simplicity and extensive community support. Python serves as the cornerstone for AI development, facilitating seamless integration with various libraries and frameworks essential for ML and deep learning tasks.

Integral to the development process are integrated development environments (IDEs) such as PyCharm and Jupyter Notebooks. These platforms offer a user-friendly interface for coding, testing, and debugging AI algorithms efficiently. Additionally, the installation of requisite libraries and frameworks, including TensorFlow and PyTorch, is imperative. These libraries provide a plethora of tools and functionalities indispensable for building and training sophisticated AI models.

Furthermore, hardware considerations are paramount, particularly regarding computational resources. Depending on the scale and complexity of the projects, developers may necessitate high-performance graphics processing units (GPUs) to expedite the training process of ML models. GPUs, renowned for their parallel processing capabilities, significantly enhance the speed and efficiency of AI computations, particularly for tasks involving complex neural network architectures and large datasets.

Establishing an optimal development environment involves a judicious selection of software tools and hardware resources tailored to the specific requirements of AI projects. By leveraging Python as the programming language of choice, coupled with robust IDEs and GPU-accelerated computing, developers can create an environment conducive to innovation and productivity in the dynamic field of AI.

INTRODUCTION TO PYTHON FOR AI

Python stands as the undisputed lingua franca for AI development, owing to its readability, versatility, and the extensive ecosystem of libraries it supports. For beginners venturing into the realm of AI, mastering Python basics is paramount. This entails familiarizing oneself with Python syntax, fundamental commands, and essential data structures like lists, tuples, and dictionaries.

In the context of AI development, proficiency in key libraries is indispensable. NumPy, for instance, is instrumental for performing numerical operations and managing multidimensional arrays, a fundamental aspect of ML and data analysis. Pandas, alternately, facilitates efficient data manipulation and analysis, providing powerful tools for data preprocessing and exploration. Additionally, Matplotlib emerges as a cornerstone for data visualization, enabling developers to create insightful visual representations of their data with ease.

Python's simplicity and elegance alleviate the learning curve for aspiring AI developers. By abstracting away complex syntax intricacies, Python empowers practitioners to focus on experimenting with AI concepts and building innovative solutions. Moreover, the supportive Python community serves as an invaluable resource for novices, offering a plethora of tutorials, documentation, and online forums for guidance and troubleshooting. This collaborative environment fosters a culture of learning and knowledge-sharing, enabling individuals to rapidly progress in their AI journey and overcome challenges encountered along the way.

Python's ubiquity in the AI landscape stems from its accessibility, versatility, and robustness. Aspiring AI developers stand to benefit immensely from harnessing Python's capabilities, leveraging its rich ecosystem of libraries and resources to embark on their journey toward mastering AI.

USING POPULAR AI LIBRARIES

This section delves into pivotal AI libraries and frameworks that play a pivotal role in the development of AI applications. TensorFlow, an offering from Google, stands out for its versatile ecosystem comprising tools, libraries, and a vibrant community, empowering researchers to pioneer advancements in ML and facilitating developers in seamlessly constructing and deploying ML-powered applications.

In contrast, PyTorch, spearheaded by Facebook, introduces dynamic computational graphing, a feature that enables flexibility in modifying model architecture. This attribute makes PyTorch the preferred choice for projects necessitating adaptability to varying requirements and experimental approaches.

Beyond these flagship frameworks, other notable libraries like Scikit-learn and Keras merit exploration for their utility in AI development. Scikit-learn, revered for its user-friendly interface, simplifies the implementation of standard ML algorithms such as regression, clustering, and classification. Keras, however, offers a high-level neural networks application programming interface (API), streamlining the process of building and experimenting with neural network architectures.

Each of these libraries and frameworks contributes uniquely to the AI landscape, addressing diverse needs and preferences of developers and researchers. While TensorFlow and PyTorch dominate the arena with their robust features and extensive support, Scikit-learn and Keras cater to practitioners seeking simplicity and efficiency in implementing ML algorithms and neural network models. By harnessing the capabilities of these libraries, AI enthusiasts can embark on ambitious projects, innovate with innovative techniques, and contribute to the advancement of AI.

AI APPLICATION: SET UP AN AI DEVELOPMENT ENVIRONMENT AND RUN A BASIC PYTHON SCRIPT

In this AI application, readers will set up an AI development environment using Python and Jupyter Notebook and run a simple AI-related Python script. This guide provides step-by-step instructions to ensure users can follow along easily.

- *Step 1*: Install Python

- *Step 2*: Install Jupyter Notebook

- *Step 3*: Set Up a Virtual Environment (Optional but Recommended)

- *Step 4*: Create and Run a Jupyter Notebook

Step 1: Install Python

1. Download Python:

   - Go to the [official Python Web site] (*https://www.python.org/downloads/*).

   - Download the latest version of Python for the operating system being used (Windows, macOS, or Linux).

2. Install Python:

   - Run the installer and follow the on-screen instructions.

   - Make sure to check the box that says "Add Python to PATH" during the installation process.

3. Verify Installation:

- Open a terminal or command prompt.

- Type "python --version" and press Enter.

- The installed Python version will be displayed.

```
C:\Users\erik>python --version
Python 3.11.4
```

Step 2: Install Jupyter Notebook

1. Install Jupyter Notebook:

- Open a terminal or command prompt.

- Type "pip install notebook" and press Enter.

- Wait for the installation to complete.

2. Verify Installation:

- Type "jupyter notebook" and press Enter.

- A Web browser should open with the Jupyter Notebook interface.

Step 3: Set Up a Virtual Environment (Optional but Recommended)

1. Create a Virtual Environment:

- Open a terminal or command prompt.

- Navigate to the directory where project will be created.

- Type "python -m venv myenv" and press Enter (replace "myenv" with desired environment name).

2. Activate the Virtual Environment:

- On Windows:

- Type "myenv\Scripts\activate" and press Enter.

- On macOS/Linux:

- Type "source myenv/bin/activate" and press Enter.

3. Install Jupyter Notebook in the Virtual Environment:

   • With the virtual environment activated, type "pip install note-book" and press Enter.

Step 4: Create and Run a Jupyter Notebook

1. Launch Jupyter Notebook:

   • In the terminal or command prompt, type "jupyter notebook" and press Enter.

   • A Web browser should open with the Jupyter Notebook interface.

2. Create a New Notebook:

   • In the Jupyter Notebook interface, click on "New" and select "Python 3."

   • A new notebook will open.

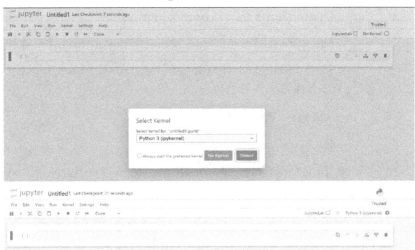

3. Run a Simple AI-Related Python Script:

- Copy and paste the following Python script into the first cell of the notebook:

```
import numpy as np
from sklearn.linear_model import LinearRegression
import matplotlib.pyplot as plt

X = np.array([[1], [2], [3], [4], [5]])
y = np.array([1, 4, 9, 16, 25])

model = LinearRegression()
model.fit(X, y)

X_new = np.array([[6], [7], [8]])
y_pred = model.predict(X_new)

plt.scatter(X, y, color='blue', label='Actual data')
plt.plot(X_new, y_pred, color='red', label='Model predictions')
plt.xlabel('X')
plt.ylabel('y')
plt.legend()
plt.show()
```

- Click "Run" or press "Shift + Enter" to execute the cell.

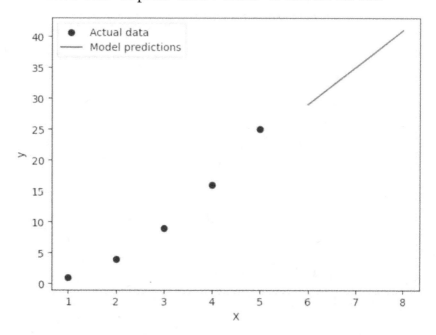

4. Understand the Script

- The script imports necessary libraries: "numpy" for numerical operations, "sklearn" for ML, and "matplotlib" for plotting.

- It generates some sample data and trains a linear regression model.

- It then makes predictions using the trained model and plots the actual data and the model's predictions.

Following these steps enables users to successfully set up an AI development environment and run a simple AI-related Python script using Jupyter Notebook. This foundational setup will allow users to experiment with various AI and ML projects.

CONCLUSION

This chapter not only guides the reader through the technical setup and essentials of Python programming, but also through leveraging powerful libraries to build and experiment with AI models. This foundational knowledge is geared toward enabling readers to start their AI journey, experimenting with projects, and potentially contributing to innovative solutions in the field of AI.

OVERVIEW OF THE LISP PROGRAMMING LANGUAGE

isp, short for "List Processing," is one of the oldest high-level programming languages and has had a profound impact on the development of artificial intelligence (AI) and computer science. Created by John McCarthy in 1958, Lisp was designed to facilitate symbolic computation, which is essential for AI research. Its unique features and powerful capabilities have made it a staple in AI and many other fields.

KEY FEATURES OF LISP

Symbolic Expression (S-Expressions)

Lisp's primary data structure is the symbolic expression, or S-expression, which can represent both code and data. This uniform representation simplifies the manipulation of code and data, making it easier to write programs that generate and modify other programs.

Recursive Functions

Lisp was one of the first languages to support recursive functions, allowing functions to call themselves. This feature is crucial for many AI algorithms, particularly those involving recursive data structures like trees and lists.

Dynamic Typing

Variables in Lisp are dynamically typed, meaning that their types are determined at runtime. This flexibility allows for rapid prototyping and experimentation, which are essential in AI research.

Garbage Collection

Lisp was among the first programming languages to implement automatic garbage collection, which helps manage memory by reclaiming unused memory, thus preventing memory leaks and other related issues.

Macros

One of Lisp's most powerful features is its macro system, which allows developers to create new syntactic constructs in a way that is almost indistinguishable from the language's core syntax. Macros enable the creation of highly expressive and concise code, fostering greater abstraction and code reuse.

IMPACT ON AI AND COMPUTER SCIENCE

Lisp's design has had a lasting influence on the field of AI. Its ability to handle symbolic information and perform complex symbolic manipulations made it the language of choice for many early AI projects. Lisp's flexibility and extensibility also allowed researchers to experiment with new ideas and techniques, contributing significantly to the advancement of AI.

Some notable AI systems and projects that have utilized Lisp include:

- SHRDLU: An early natural language understanding program developed by Terry Winograd in the 1960s.

- Macsyma: A pioneering computer algebra system.

- Common Lisp: An evolution of the original Lisp, standardized to unify various dialects and provide a comprehensive set of features for modern AI research.

MODERN USE AND LEGACY

While newer languages like Python have become more popular in AI research and development due to their extensive libraries and ease of use, Lisp continues to be valued for its unique capabilities. It remains a preferred choice for certain specialized AI applications, academic research, and projects requiring highly abstract or symbolic computation.

The principles and paradigms introduced by Lisp, such as functional programming and the use of garbage collection, have been incorporated into many modern programming languages. Lisp's influence is evident in languages like Python, JavaScript, and Ruby, which adopt some of its key features and philosophies.

In summary, Lisp's innovative approach to programming has left an indelible mark on AI and computer science. Its emphasis on symbolic computation, recursion, dynamic typing, garbage collection, and macros has shaped the development of programming languages and continues to inspire new generations of developers and researchers.

RESOURCES AND COMMUNITY

The field of AI is vast and constantly evolving, making continuous learning and community engagement crucial for anyone interested in this area. This appendix serves as a comprehensive guide to a wealth of resources available for both novices and seasoned practitioners. This chapter covers the best online courses, insightful tutorials, and must-read books that can help deepen the reader's understanding of AI. Additionally, this chapter highlights vibrant AI communities and forums where one can share knowledge, collaborate on projects, and connect with peers. This chapter not only directs readers to where they can learn more about AI, but it also helps one navigate the extensive network of AI enthusiasts and professionals worldwide, fostering a collaborative and informed AI community.

ONLINE COURSES AND TUTORIALS

With the proliferation of online learning platforms, there are numerous courses available that cater to all levels of AI expertise. Highlight top platforms like Coursera, edX, and Udacity, which offer courses developed in collaboration with leading universities and tech companies. For instance, Coursera's "Machine Learning" course by Andrew Ng from Stanford University is a highly recommended starting point for beginners. For more practical, hands-on learning, platforms like DataCamp and Codecademy offer interactive tutorials that focus on implementing AI concepts through coding exercises and mini-projects. These courses cover a range of topics from basic data science skills to advanced machine learning and neural network programming.

AI COMMUNITIES AND FORUMS

Active participation in AI communities and forums is crucial for staying updated with the latest developments and networking with other AI professionals. Discuss prominent online communities such as Stack Overflow, GitHub, and Reddit, which host vibrant discussions, project collaborations, and peer-to-peer support. Highlight specialized forums like the Machine Learning subreddit or specific groups on LinkedIn and Facebook that focus on niche areas within AI. Additionally, mention the importance of attending AI conferences, hackathons, and meetups such as NeurIPS, ICML (International Conference on Machine Learning), and local Tech Talks, which provide opportunities to learn from and network with thought leaders and innovators in the field.

RECOMMENDED BOOKS AND JOURNALS

Books and academic journals remain invaluable resources for those looking to deepen their understanding of AI. Recommend essential reads such as *Artificial Intelligence: A Modern Approach* by Stuart Russell and Peter Norvig, which is widely regarded as the definitive text on the theory and practice of AI. For those interested in the implications of AI on society and ethics, suggest *Weapons of Math Destruction* by Cathy O'Neil. Highlight leading journals such as the *Journal of Artificial Intelligence Research (JAIR)* and the *Artificial Intelligence Journal (AIJ)* that publish peer-reviewed research papers offering cutting-edge insights into current AI research and applications.

Index

www.ingramcontent.com/pod-product-compliance
Lightning Source LLC
La Vergne TN
LVHW022316060326
832902LV00020B/3503